JOURNEY OF
LIGHT

JOURNEY OF LIGHT

Stories of Dawn

After Darkness

PETER SHOCKEY AND STOWE D. SHOCKEY

DOUBLEDAY

New York   London   Toronto   Sydney   Auckland

PUBLISHED BY DOUBLEDAY

Published in the United States by Doubleday, an imprint of The Doubleday Broadway Publishing Group, a division of Random House, Inc., New York.
www.doubleday.com

DOUBLEDAY and the portrayal of an anchor with a dolphin are registered trademarks of Random House, Inc.

Permissions appear on p. 249.

Book design by Chris Welch

Library of Congress Cataloging-in-Publication Data
Shockey, Peter.
Journey of light : stories of dawn after darkness / Peter Shockey and Stowe D. Shockey. — 1st ed.
p. cm.
1. Christian life. I. Shockey, Stowe. II. Title.
BV4515.3.S56 2007
242—dc22
2006023676

ISBN 978-0-385-50126-2

PRINTED IN THE UNITED STATES OF AMERICA

1   3   5   7   9   10   8   6   4   2

First Edition

Written for our daughters,
Christina Leigh Shockey
and
Grace Caroline Shockey

May this be a help in finding
the Light within you,
to guide you
on your own journeys . . .

We are living in a world that is absolutely transparent, and God is shining through it all the time.

—Thomas Merton

CONTENTS

Acknowledgments   XIII

Introduction   XV

PART I
A DARK WORLD

Chapter 1   Disconnected from God   3

Chapter 2   An Imperfect World   12

Chapter 3   Spiritual Challenge   25

Chapter 4   The Separated Self   35

Chapter 5   Our Fallen Nature   43

Chapter 6   Abandoned and Alone   53

PART II
SEARCHLIGHTS OF HOPE

Chapter 7   A Light in the Darkness   61

Chapter 8   The Impenetrable Wall   68

Chapter 9   Wrestling with God   80

Chapter 10   A Place to Grow   89

Chapter 11   The Path to Perfect Union   102

Chapter 12   An Open Door to the Past   122

PART III
RECONNECTING TO THE LIGHT

Chapter 13   Healing Revelations   131

Chapter 14   Crossing the Bitter Bridge   138

Chapter 15   Seeds of Forgiveness   144

Chapter 16   The Healing Begins   153

Chapter 17   Reconnecting: Body, Mind,
and Spirit   167

PART IV
CONNECTIONS AND CONCLUSIONS

Chapter 18   Power and Light for
the Journey   181

Chapter 19   Conduits of God's Healing
Light   201

Chapter 20   Afterlife Experiences and
the Ripple Effect   215

Chapter 21   **The Ripple Effect**   234

Epilogue   **Thanksgiving and Praise**   240

Notes   245

Permissions   249

ACKNOWLEDGMENTS

First we want to thank The Light of the World for entering our hearts when we invited Him so many years ago.

We would also like to express our thanks to all those who were instrumental in the creation and completion of this book.

To Joe Durepos for his tireless representation. To Trace Murphy for his steadfast encouragement. To Angela DePriest, for her gifted editorial craftsmanship. To Andrew Corbin for his positive support.

Thanks to the many reviewers and proofreaders who took time to reflect and advise us through the course of this literary journey: Jamie Chavez; Teresa Whitehurst; Michael and Margarita Noyes; Dan DePriest; Eric Link; Gene Smith; Fred Rowles; and Joyce Peck.

And we want to give our grateful appreciation to all of

those people who have shared their stories with us over the years. Your stories have made this tapestry possible.

Finally, we send our greatest love and thanks to Manon Shockey, and to all our parents whom we are eager to see again in heaven, so we can continue sharing the stories of what the Light has done, both here and there.

Peter and Stowe Shockey

INTRODUCTION

I had just finished an especially stressful day of work, trying to wrap up a job for a new client using my computerized video editing system. It was the proverbial trip to *computer h-e-l-l,* where it seemed that no matter what I did, I received messages like "File not found," or "Exceptional access error violation," or the most diabolical, "Fatal error." It was the kind of day when there is no mercy; I was being judged *by the letter of the law.* Computers are legalistic and coldhearted that way. Every iota, every jot, every last little logical bit of information must be exactly so; if not, you are punished by watching your entire system seize and convulse like a wretched animal, and you fight the urge to put the beast out of its misery. Your own nerve endings prickle with helpless panic because you suspect it's your fault, and yet you don't know what to do to make it right. The whole system just dies because something somewhere is disconnected. It has to be one of modern life's best metaphors for *the wages of sin!*

So I was recovering from one of the worst of those kinds of days when I got a phone call from a friend named Jeannie Hunter. I had interviewed Jeannie several years earlier to document a miraculous healing she had experienced, and we have remained in touch. What she was about to tell me would remind me of why in the world I chose to go into such a technically demanding business as filmmaking.

Jeannie had just received a call from an out-of-town coworker, and she called to share with me what she'd heard. She explained that a year earlier the coworker had lent one of my documentaries to a troubled young woman at her office—a woman who was suffering from an abusive and raging husband. The video showed Jeannie's own miraculous healing when God reconnected her facial nerves—which had been accidentally severed during surgery and left her with a loss of equilibrium, partial deafness, and no sensation of taste. Jeannie's friend had hoped to use the video to gently open the door to the young woman's heart so she could then introduce her to God's ability to mend lives. As it turned out, the girl was deeply moved when she watched Jeannie's story and did indeed open up to a conversation that led to great healing in her own life.

Jeannie said, "That young girl came to know the Lord personally because she was touched through your film. She managed to get her life back on track, learned to trust God, and developed a real joyful attitude about life."

I don't often hear that kind of enthusiastic reaction to my films because of the anonymous nature of television; so I was lifted by hearing it and thanked Jeannie for telling me.

But then she said, "Well, that's not the end of the story. My associate called me last night to inform me that the young lady was shot to death by her ex-husband two days ago."

I was stunned. What could I say? I stammered, "Oh, I am so sorry. . . ."

"Peter," Jeannie quickly added, "don't forget that this girl *did* get the healing she needed. She had already found her peace with God, and she's resting in His presence now."

My mind raced with open-ended questions about the harshness of life, about past problems that don't seem to go away, and about the sudden end to the young lady's life story. And yet I also knew that what Jeannie said is true: God is ultimately concerned with the health of our soul, and everything else is temporary. Our time here is like a brief flowering in the garden. The Lord's love for us extends much deeper and more eternally than we can possibly see from here.

Suddenly my thoughts scanned back to the scene of my sick computer and the strange similarity to a life disconnected from God. My machine had suffered from a confusing mess of bad information, corrupted files, and hardware conflicts. It was not operating in the way it was originally created to function. The only way that I could find a remedy for the symptoms was to contact the manufacturer for help. Ultimately, I was advised to disconnect the unauthorized peripheral hardware (things I had personally added to the system, ignorant of their harmful effects), then to reinstall the software and reconnect everything properly—which meant I needed to begin again. That took care of the root of my problems, essentially fixing the system.

The fellow from technical support had scoured his database for other cases similar to mine that had been reported and then prescribed what the solutions had been. That collection of experiences gave me confidence that I could trust the consultant to provide correct answers to my problem.

Extending the parallel, the tech support's database is similar to collecting and sharing stories about people's miraculous experiences. Stories of God's healing power provide confidence and courage for readers to put their trust in Him, too. These stories remind us that the Lord loves us and wants us to operate at our best capacity. The stories themselves—connecting people to God's Holy and healing Light—are inspiring and strangely contagious! One person's story enlightens another person's faith and inspires healing, which in turn touches the hearts of others and builds their faith as well.

Many of the stories in this book have been collected from people whose lives have influenced ours—by wisdom gained from their experiences. Occasionally we encountered someone who shared with us a precious sketchbook of their most touching memories. In them we uncovered lovingly rendered portraits of such skillful beauty that to behold them still invokes sweet twinges of pain and remembrance in our own hearts.

And that's how my wife, Stowe, came to that deepest place where her own painful memories were revealed—opened wide like a Pandora's box, terrifying and captivating—for the world to see. But I didn't see Stowe's pain when we met; all I saw was the woman with whom I wanted to spend the rest of my life.

It was seventeen years ago that I climbed into the backseat of my friend Gene's Isuzu Trooper. He had invited me on a blind double-date with two pretty ladies, one of whom he *thought* I might be interested in meeting. Charlu was a glamorous blond who dressed in head-turning, form-fitting outfits. But as soon as I saw her friend, Stowe—also beautiful, but not quite as splashy—I somehow recognized her and fell instantly in love!

She and I sat next to each other at the movie *The Dream Team,* and we talked through the entire show. A little more than one year later we were married—one of the very best decisions I have ever made. Eventually, Christina Leigh and Grace Caroline were born to us, two years apart, and they also rank among the greatest blessings granted by God. Every once in a while—now with such a wonderful family—I ask myself this question: *If I died tomorrow, what legacy would I leave to them?*

One day, as Stowe and I pondered the question together, we realized that we possess nearly one hundred years of collective life experiences (I am fifty-one and she is forty-six), and that our little girls will inherit the wisdom of those experiences because of our *partnership.* Also, realizing that a beautiful marriage like ours is something to be cherished in today's world, it seemed fitting that we create a ledger together—a kind of treasure chest into which we can put our most valuable thoughts, memories, and stories—good and bad.

You see, when my friend Gene introduced me to Stowe, it was not an isolated, random event; the ripples of that moment will continue through generations, which not only connect Gene to my own legacy, but me to his and exponentially outward to everyone we touch.

There are jewels of wisdom in this book and, as you'll learn from Stowe's experiences, not all the stories are bright ones. Many are the result of learning from episodes of both light and dark, joys and frustrations, pain and recovery. Being human includes a great deal of suffering, doubting, and terrible struggling to make the right choices, all while living in this confusing world. I know our children's lives will be filled with similar highs and lows, but I hope they can learn from some of the experiences of others who went before them. Whatever their paths, I believe that their journeys, like our own, will be journeys to Light.

Journey of Light is a story of God's healing Light. Each chapter is narrated against the bittersweet backdrop of Stowe's dramatic past, traveling and rippling through the dense world of her losses, blocked by her fears, absorbed by her pains, and deflected by her doubts—only to reunite her with Him, victoriously, at the other end of a tragic tale, which is only the *middle* of her life's story.

The Light we refer to in the title is, of course, God—the origin of all creation. *God is Light!* Jesus said it of Himself, *"I am the Light of the world,"* and He also said it of each of us, *"You are the Light of the World . . . let your Light shine before men. . . ."* The Light of God is what connects everything to everything; and sharing that Light, generously and lovingly, is the way to heal all broken connections whether spiritual, physical, or emotional.

People I've interviewed who had returned from near-death experiences often refer to a phenomenon known as the *ripple effect*. Upon seeing their life "flash before their eyes," they gain an immediate understanding of how everyone's lives impinge upon one another . . . like so many ripples from a pebble cast into a pond, radiating out to touch those in their circle of influence. It seems that each person's life can have a penetrating effect on others, either positively or negatively. And it demonstrates how vitally connected to one another we are. So, consciously or not, we are deeply and eternally connected to one another, to God, and to His entire Cosmos. Everything we do affects the world around us in profound ways, both good and bad, just as we are affected by the deeds of others. No actions are without reactions; no energy is ever lost; and no one is ever really alone. We make this journey together toward one destination—not to a place, but to a person—Jesus Christ. We journey through this life on our way to becoming like Him and sharing eternity with Him and those who also know Him.

In this book you will see many examples of how one person's decision to share God's Light touched countless others, thus illustrating the power of its ability to heal and reconnect.

Jesus himself told those whom He cured, *"Your* faith *has made you well"* (Matt. 9:22 ESV; emphasis mine); and while His reputation for healing spread through the land, more and more people put their *faith* in His ability to touch them, too.

That young woman, the friend of Jeannie's coworker, whose heart had been rescued from her suffering, handed down her story of healing to enlighten other people's hearts, such as mine. Once again, I can see our links to one another. I've come to believe that it is vital to share these stories of healing, in order to assure our spiritual reconnection so we can clearly transmit God's Light.

We know within our hearts that God will greet us at the end of the journey, proud of our learning and forgiving of our failings. After all, this is not so much our own journey, but the journey of *His Light*—in us and through us.

And this, our logbook of that journey of Light, is our legacy to pass along to the world.

Peter Shockey
May 2006

PART I
A DARK WORLD

CHAPTER ONE

DISCONNECTED FROM GOD

For it is the God who commanded light to shine out
of darkness, who has shone in our hearts to give the
light of the knowledge of the glory of God in the
face of Jesus Christ.

—2 COR. 4:6 NKJV

Stowe's Journey

I squinted my eyes in the midmorning light of a perfect spring day. I could hardly resist the urge to stop and take it all in. Leaning against my hoe, I looked on while my husband, Peter, worked. He was busy weeding, planting, and doing what he enjoys so much: making our yard a paradise. Over in the plastic pool, giggling uncontrollably, were our girls, Christina and Grace. *What a beautiful sight.* I breathed in deeply.

I had come a long way to arrive at this moment in time. My heart was full of thankfulness to God. We were all healthy, the sun was shining—life was definitely good.

Suddenly my thoughts were interrupted by a distant phone ringing. Dropping the hoe, I made a mad dash to the house. I had no idea at that moment that my life was about to change course—once again—for the call I was running to answer wasn't just *any* call; it was "the" call. You know the kind; it raps loudly on the window of your soul, reminding you that there's more to life than just work, play, and, in our case, gardening. *Get moving now*, it urges. *You have a purpose here on earth. Time is much shorter than you think. Be still. Listen.*

I caught the phone just before my answering machine interrupted. "Hello," I said, cheerfully albeit somewhat out of breath.

"Stowe," the raspy voice sounded distressed. "I just came back from the doctor. . . . I have inoperable lung cancer."

I fell back onto the nearest chair. "What?" I whispered. I could barely speak.

"The doctor says with chemo and radiation I might live a year to a year and a half. Without it—maybe six months."

We hung on the phone a few more minutes, consoling each other as the news sank in. And then, with plans to get together later that day, we said our good-byes. "I love you, Dad. . . ." *Click.*

Except for the sound of my heavy breath, all was silent. Cloaked in the cool darkness of our basement rec room, I sat there totally stunned. Outside, in our backyard, the world was still sunny, untouched by this latest news. Inside, however, our lives had once again turned on a dime. *This can't be happening. Was cancer going to kill another parent?* At seventy-two, Dad was not in the greatest of shape. He had several major things wrong with him, including diabetes, heart disease, and cirrhosis of the liver. In fact, his health was one of the main reasons he had decided to move to Nashville only a year earlier. He wanted to be closer to us . . . just in case. Still, even knowing he had all these strikes against him, it was hard for me to believe this was happening.

I thought of Peter; I needed to tell him. Walking somberly into the bright sunlight, I went to him, broke the news, and took comfort in his loving arms. There, under the blue sky, we held each other and cried.

Four days after that fateful phone call I had a dream—a dream I believe was sent from God. I awoke with Peter's arms around me, consoling me and saying, "It's all right . . . you're okay . . . you were just having a bad dream."

But it *wasn't* just a dream. It was a memory from my subconscious—a wake-up call. But just for a moment, I was still there, in the middle of one of the most memorable and vivid dreams I have ever experienced:

I was shopping in a discount store and had laid my purse down when I noticed a woman picking it up and taking it. I immediately went to her. "Hey, that's my purse," I said. She slowly turned around and reluctantly gave it back to me. She looked like a sad woman, worn down by life and bad circumstances, maybe someone on drugs. But as I studied her a little more, I realized she looked familiar. "Debra?" I asked tentatively.

For just a moment our eyes met. "Yes," she softly answered.

"Weren't you and I in a home together?"

"Yeah." She was staring down at the ground now.

"Well, how's it going?"

She took a shallow breath and said, "Not too good . . . I don't have any money."

"Oh, well, I've got a few dollars you can have," I said,

pulling out my wallet and opening it toward her. She reached out, grabbed the money, and left —no thanks, no good-bye. I watched as she walked away, thinking about what a miserable life she must have. Then I looked back down into my wallet. "Oh, no!" She had taken my credit card!

I raced through the store and caught up with her outside in a sunny courtyard area. She was sitting at a table. "Uh, Debra, I think you accidentally took my credit card. May I have it back?"

Diverting her eyes from mine, she said, "I don't have your credit card. Leave me alone!"

What could I do? I felt so helpless. I wandered over to a picnic table and sat down in an area where the sun was intensely bright. Then, placing my arms on the table, I began to cry the tears of a victim; but as they fell, something strange caught my eye. There in the bright sunshine I saw writing and pictures on my arms. They were etched in white, which fascinated me. How did they get there? I wondered. Why are they white? I could not quite make out exactly what was on my left arm, but what I saw on my right arm shook me at the center of my soul. In bold white letters, it read, I AM AN ABUSED CHILD.

And I began to cry.

✳

Peter

I was driving along, talking with a client on my hands-free cell phone, when suddenly . . . total silence. Our signal was cut off as I drove through a "dead zone."

Our lives are exactly like that every few miles of our epic journey. Everything is going along so well, we are feeling good, and suddenly "Hello? *HELLO?*" It seems like we are cut off from God and from the continuous flow of life as we spend the next little while trying to reconnect.

I don't think it matters how smart, how successful, how spiritual, or how sincere a person is—everyone is going to be regularly thrown a detour in life that forces them to take inventory of their past, present, and future. These events are what make our life story into a compelling journey, with all the dramatic elements of tension, plot twists, character development, and ultimately a climactic resolution where we eternally reconnect to that which we have been seeking all along.

> *We have not received the spirit of the world but the*
> *Spirit who is from God, that we may understand*
> *what God has freely given us. This is what we*
> *speak, not in words taught us by human wisdom*
> *but in words taught by the Spirit, expressing spiri-*
> *tual truths in spiritual words.*
> —1 COR. 2:12–13 NIV

Stowe

I was sitting in my favorite rocking chair and taking in the solitude of a new day when I glanced over at my Bible lying open on the table. I was drawn to the above passage in 1 Corinthians, and as I read I felt a little jolt of excitement, for I realized Paul was telling us that we have been given the Spirit of God—we should have a direct connection with Him, and we should know His very thoughts. What an incredible gift! To know God's will, even hear His voice—in short, to be connected with the Almighty!

But as I pondered those words, I couldn't help but wonder how many people feel that they share that kind of connection with God. Only rarely have I felt anything close to that kind of bond, and I'm fairly sure I am not alone.

WHERE IS GOD?

So I was left with this question: If the spirit is our inheritance from God, why do so many of us find ourselves sitting quietly in a darkened room with a heavy heart, not only feeling disconnected from God but, in fact, alienated from Him? I recalled that, over and over in conversations with people, I have heard things like, "How do I know God's will for me?"; "How do I know if God is talking to me?"; and "Is God even listening to me?" The answer *sounds* simple; even if putting it into practice is one of the hardest things to do: If our relationship with God is strong—if we are in complete harmony with Him—we would know in our hearts His will for us; we would sense His voice speaking to us; and we would feel His Spirit listening to us.

Let me put it to you this way: How often have you known someone so "in tune" with you that you knew their thoughts even before they spoke? Or perhaps an image of that special person crosses your mind and then suddenly the phone rings and you hear that person's voice? Those kinds of relationships, in which our hearts and minds seem to be on the same wavelength, usually come about through a genuine heart connection—but they grow and blossom because of the amount of time we spend together and because of the depth to which we want to truly *know* a person.

When I look at my life and the lives of others, it's really not surprising why so many people have a disconnected relationship with God, which in turn can lead to a disconnection with our fellow humans. It seems we too often leave out the *relat-ing* part of our relationships. Our prayers, when we remember to say them, sound more like a quick wish list followed by an "amen," and then off to work or play we go. Can you imagine a marriage where one person talks all the time, asking favors of their spouse, then says, "Let it be," and just walks out of the room? It would end in a quick divorce. No, a good relationship requires communication on both sides.

So with that in mind, how much time each day do we spend with the people in this world who matter most to us—an hour or two, maybe three? Now, how much time each day do we spend in prayer or meditation—talking and, more important, just listening to God—an hour or possibly two? Sadly, for most of us, a more realistic answer would probably be a few minutes a day. At best, that's all we spend in conversation with our magnificent Creator. We often find ourselves saying, "I'm just too busy," and yet we spend copious amounts of time with people, TVs, computers, and all sorts of other activities.

Maybe this explains why we have so many unanswered questions about God. Perhaps it is the reason we fail to hear our Heavenly Father's voice whispering to us over the din of our daily lives. How can we recognize the voice of someone we never listen to?

By not staying in touch with God, we will inevitably ques-tion His presence in our lives and wander aimlessly like a lost child in the dark. And when we fail to seek Him for direction on a regular basis, we soon discover ourselves going in circles. Panic sets in, and our childish inner voices begin leading us astray, making it even harder to hear the beckoning call of our Father. And just at the moment when we need Him most, we become doubtful that God can even hear us. We may even feel guilty about begging for His help only when we need it.

God wants to reconnect with us; all we have to do is ask and then be willing to listen. I have learned that He is speaking to us (more often than we might think!), and not only with His *voice,* but in all sorts of other ways. He uses dreams—just as He did when He reminded me that I am an abused child—as well as pictures, media, angels, and even regular people to deliver His messages.

If we are not hearing God's voice, the first thing we might want to pray for is to simply reconnect with Him. We may ask God, in our own sincere words, to help figure out what's making us feel cut off from Him. There may be hidden doubts, negative inner voices, or hidden resentments that keep us from being in His presence. All these things need to be brought out of the shadows before we can be filled with His peaceful and compassionate Light.

Recognizing the darkness we are in, identifying the experiences that may be casting long shadows, and opening up our hearts to God's Light are the surest ways of reuniting our spirit with His. And if we are looking for answers, we should try asking questions.

He is waiting for us. No matter where we are in life, He is there—in our joy, in our sadness, in our laughter, in our losses. In fact, some of us have our biggest "God moments" in times of deepest sorrow. We have a sincere need to hear from Him when we are afraid and, at last, cry out to Him: "God, I can't do this anymore by myself. . . . Help me!" or, "Where are you, Lord? Why don't you hear me?" It is in these times of great need that we are putting Him to the test and asking something of Him. And I believe God always responds to sincere need.

Just like the compassionate and respectful marriage that Peter and I share, the marriage of our human minds with God's divine Spirit must communicate our needs and desires for the good of the union. Each of us has received the Spirit of God so that we may connect with our Creator on a daily basis, to share our joys and sorrows, and to feel His incredible love. But it will never be forced upon us; He has given us free will, so connecting with His Spirit is a decision only we can make.

Unfortunately, free will also means that many of us can't always be counted on to act in our own best interest; thus the journey is a long and painful one. As a child I was at the mercy of others, and I had few choices about how my life would play out. But when I became an adult, the decisions were mine, and it still took a very long time before I reconnected with God's divine Spirit.

CHAPTER TWO

AN IMPERFECT WORLD

That is why, for Christ's sake, I delight in
weaknesses, in insults, in hardships, in persecutions,
in difficulties. For when I am weak,
then I am strong.

—2 COR. 12:10 NIV

Stowe's Journey

When I became aware of my surroundings, I was at home in our bed—it was 5:00 A.M. But those white-lettered words, I AM AN ABUSED CHILD, were branded on my conscience and I could not stop crying. Peter immediately rolled over and, like the good husband and friend he is, held me as I wept. And then he listened as I told him my dream.

Now the words were on the table—I had spoken them out loud. Gone were the days of pretending as though my past had been just a slight inconvenience. I had to face it— I was an abused child. And so began the first step in the healing process—learning, at long last, how to grieve.

I spent most of that Saturday in a tearful trance, somewhat removed from reality. That night, however, we were scheduled to visit some friends out in the country, and even though I didn't feel like socializing I finally agreed to go. *Maybe it will be relaxing*, I thought.

We hadn't been at our friend's house too long when I noticed my hands were beginning to itch. At first I thought it might just be mosquitoes or possibly poison ivy. I didn't pay much attention to it that night, but by the next morning my fingers were itching, sometimes to the point of distraction.

A few days went by and a mysterious rash slowly crept up my arms. My fingers became so swollen I couldn't remove my rings, and the itching was driving me crazy. I frequently found myself at the kitchen sink, holding my hands under scalding hot water, trying to get some relief from the itching. I used creams and sprays but nothing worked. By the end of the week the rash was beginning to show up in spots on my legs. Friends and neighbors suggested different treatments, but in my heart I knew this rash came from somewhere deep within; an ugly reminder of the turmoil in my spirit.

Even though the revealing missive on my arm was clear to me, the solution was not; and I had neither the courage nor the inclination to ask God or anyone else for help. I would just have to suffer through it.

Subsequently, while I was dealing with this ugly, embarrassing rash, I also found myself slipping deeper each day into a depression. I tried to keep up a good face when taking Dad to his doctor appointments, but at home with my family it was obvious something was wrong. I became withdrawn and lost my appetite. Everyday tasks were getting harder to accomplish, and Peter was worried about me; he had seen me in this depressed state many times. But I tried to reassure him that I would get over this the same way I had always done—just wait it out. "I'll be okay," I said tearfully.

During times of depression it is common for my mind to wander back to days gone by, to replay the old tapes, to touch the old wounds—to feel the old pain. As I pulled away from my family, I found my mind going almost out of control, ricocheting from one old memory to another, drifting back through troubled waters.

I remember the sweltering summer nights of Atlanta in our small apartment, which had no air-conditioning. An outside lamp shone through the metal Venetian blinds, casting eerie shadows on the pale green walls.

At nearly two years old, I could pull myself up to a standing position in my crib. All was quiet except for the murmur of my parent's voices downstairs. Tears welled in my eyes. I was afraid, but I didn't know why. I cried louder, hoping someone, perhaps my mother, would come and comfort me. After a while, when no one came, I crawled out of my crib. For the next hour or so I cried at the top of the stairs.

This sad scenario (which must have been torturous for my parents) went on night after night for over a year. Though both of my parents were downstairs, the only one who came up was Dad. I know my crying must have driven him nearly crazy. He used every tactic he could think of to quell my tears. Some nights he tried tenderness; on other nights he would ignore me; sometimes he would get angry and yell at me. He tried putting my hands on the banister and ordering me to cry while standing up. He even dumped a glass of water on me once; but nothing worked. I needed something else. I needed *someone* else—my mother. *Why won't she come?*

Years later, though still a young girl, I loved looking through my parents' wedding album, reverently touching the plastic-covered black-and-white memories. My father's tuxedo . . . my mother's gloriously long gown . . . what a handsome couple Dick and Bette had been. I think my mother had one of the biggest smiles I've ever seen.

Their life together began in 1955 with a storybook wedding in Charlotte, North Carolina and a European honeymoon. Finally they settled down in peaceful Asheville. Young and full of dreams, they traveled the world, took in Broadway shows, and, together, furthered their political party. And, of course, they planned their family—three children was the agreed-upon number.

In May 1959 my brother Charles was born. There was great joy for Dick and Bette as they began life with their first child. That year was an exciting one. A temporary job offer took them to New York for seven months, where they happily took in the sights and Broadway shows. Their dreams were coming true.

Then they moved back to Asheville. Charles, a rambunctious little fellow, seemed to be developing normally in all areas except one—he showed a lack of response to sound. One day while Charles was playing on the floor, my father got out a pot and began banging loudly on it. Charles never turned around. Soon after, a visit with an auditory specialist confirmed their suspicions—Charles was found to be totally deaf (there was no apparent cause). This, of course, was a terrible blow to my parents; but they accepted the diagnosis and began moving on and making plans for Charles's future. My father was determined that Charles would lead as normal a life as possible.

Just two years after the birth of my brother, I arrived—

a long, skinny May baby. They named me Anne Stowe Dailey, after my great-great-grandmother, Lura Anne Stowe. The year was 1961, the beginning of a decade that would bring great change to both our family and the world. A week after I was born, my dad's father died of throat cancer.

But my parents were a fun couple. My father, especially, loved to have parties. The little corner bar in our house was always well stocked, and costume and theme parties were frequent. In fact, my earliest memory is of a party. It was sometime in my first year. I was in a playpen in the kitchen. My view was of stockings, high heels, long pants, and wing tips. The sounds of clinking glasses and happy voices filled my ears. And then, magically, someone lifted me—maybe it was my mother. Suddenly there was a sea of heads in the room. Parties. They were a very central part of my parent's lives.

At two and a half years old, Charles was smart as a whip, but he had to undergo further testing. It was decided he should attend a school for the deaf to teach him to read lips. Fortunately for my mother, they were able to find a preschool for the handicapped that was close to home.

In the fall of that year, my mother found a lump in her breast. According to the doctors, it was malignant and her only option was a mastectomy, followed by radiation treatments. The operation and treatments took place in Charlotte. She bravely left her home and family for the next three months to take her treatments. During that time my dad's mother (known to us as Lallie) came to stay, helping out in our time of need.

By the fall of 1962 our family was on the move. Charles had been accepted into the Atlanta Speech School, and my parents felt lucky to find a three-bedroom apartment right behind the school. Dad remained in Asheville as the house had not yet been sold, and there was little in the way of job prospects. Mom, of course, had her hands full holding down the fort with two little ones. It would be four months before Dad found a job in Atlanta and we were reunited.

With Charles doing well in school, Mom was able to not only take care of me, but also to pursue hobbies such as sewing, knitting, and speaking for a local ladies club. She and Dad even took a few trips.

But by the spring of 1963 my mother was feeling ill. Her back ached constantly, and that summer she was having a hard time getting around. In September she was hospitalized and put in traction for a supposed slipped disc. However, her real trouble was soon diagnosed as cancer of the liver and bones.

Family members once again came to the rescue to help care for our family as Mom began taking radioisotopes and drugs for her illness. She lost her hair and began sporting a new wig.

Despite all that was happening, her spirits remained for the most part upbeat. My dad, too, tried to maintain a positive spirit; but it was all a façade, for he had been told the truth. The doctor had informed him that his wife was dying, and yet he was advised to keep this knowledge to himself. It seems ludicrous by today's standards to ask this of someone, but this was a common practice of that time. It was a heavy burden for him to bear.

So many people who knew her have told me what a bright and beautiful spirit she was. *I wish I could remember.* I have memories of almost everyone in my life from that time—my father, my brother, our housekeeper, even the neighbors—but somehow my mind has withheld from me all but a few pictures of this young woman who loved me.

There is only one picture I can recall of her sweet face. I was sitting on the floor, just inches away from the television and the beginning of a soap opera: "Like sands through an hourglass . . ." came the announcer's voice, ". . . so are the days of our lives." And then she called my name: "Anne, how do you like the dress I've made you?" I remember seeing a pretty little pink dress and her beautiful face beaming at me—an unforgettable smile. *That's a good one.*

Most of my memories, though, are of her in the hospital, pictures from a child's point of view: her slender, fair hand hanging down from an incredibly large metal hospital bed, the smell of the air conditioner near the window, being lifted up to look at her, and finally, after our visits with her, my father and I making our way hand in hand down the long corridor of stairs—the only sound was the echo of our footsteps.

She died in September 1964. I was three years old.

*

What happens when we die?
Is there a God?
Is there an Afterlife?
Are Angels sent to help . . . in life?
If there's a Heaven . . . why are we here?
Does God send Miracles to some people . . . and not others?
If God loves me . . . why am I suffering?

Questions posed since time began . . .
At times the Divine is encountered firsthand.

To those touched, they need no more proof.
And for us—hearing stories of Divine Love—something
stirs . . .
inspiring love in return—for God—and for one another . . .
Circling back in untold ways,
intersecting our hearts,
like ripples in a pond . . .

Peter

I wrote the above lines in September 2000 as the opening for my new TV series, *Miracles, Angels & Afterlife* I felt the words spelled out the essence of my own soul-searching, which seemed to reflect that of my entire generation. I thought the statements summed up the spiritual journey that I and countless others had been on for many years. And they embodied my personal dream of producing a weekly TV series that would bring inspiring and uplifting real-life stories to people in the hearts of their dens and living rooms.

A SILENT CASUALTY

Miracles, Angels & Afterlife began as a great success in the Odyssey Channel's television ratings department. Unfortunately, the subsequent sale of a majority share of the network to the Hallmark Channel didn't help our cause, because the new management would soon steer away from Odyssey's religious image. As my coproducers and I waited for the anticipated green light for a new season of our show, we were told that the final word would come "in a week or two." But the "week or two" lasted over six months!

Meanwhile, our airtime was rescheduled in the no-man's-land of early Sunday morning and, naturally, the ratings plummeted. Then, after remaining uncommitted and thereby unemployed for more than half a year, I got word that a final decision would be made at a big meeting on Thursday, September 13, 2001.

As we prayed about the appointed meeting, my executive producer, William Spencer Reilly, readied himself in his fifteenth-floor office of Faith & Values Media, located at 74 Trinity Place—a couple of blocks from New York's Twin Towers. On Tuesday, in the face of great excitement and anticipation for the final verdict on the life of our show, and for other inspirational shows on the network, something unexpected happened.

Bill stared out his window and saw what looked like ticker-tape confetti, like one would see after a World Series victory, raining from the sky. He buzzed his associate in the next office to inquire if there was a celebration scheduled. Then, all at once, they said in unison, "It's on fire!" A burning sheet of paper landed on Bill's windowsill, and he reached out to grab it. It bore the letterhead from the great financial company, Morgan Stanley.

In the moments that followed, the entire world changed. When the towers fell, darkness enveloped Faith & Values, and for the next five hours Bill Reilly and all his associates struggled to stay alive. When the long day was finally finished, the lives of thousands were over, and the futures of those left behind were forever altered.

Faith & Values Media was uprooted from its offices for the next four months while their building was used as one of the focal points for Ground Zero cleanup. New television projects were put on hold, and in that time—along with untold numbers of casualties in business and industry—the tides turned decisively against our show.

Meanwhile, Stowe and I had been up to our ears in building a new home for our family and treaded water for those unemployed months by "hiring ourselves" to do construction work on the house. After September 2001 came and went, we continued to undertake more and more construction duties until we found ourselves virtually finishing the house ourselves; painting, siding, trim carpentry, landscaping—you name it, we did it. Anywhere we could spend construction money on our own labors, we would learn those necessary skills.

What began as an economic necessity soon became a wonderful bonding experience for our family. As we lived for nearly a year in a tiny cabin we built out of a barn, my wife and I worked dawn to dusk on the new farmhouse. Our two daughters, Christina, age six, and Grace, age four, played on the huge dirt piles and in the creek beds of our new farmland. In many ways we felt like pioneers. And for us, as on any new frontier, life was filled with uncertainty.

EVERY MAN'S QUESTIONS

Suddenly I was faced with a whole new list of soul-searching questions, unlike the ones of a year before, colored by the darkness of the unpredictable world we had entered into. On a global scale, I wondered:

- Faced by wicked men, intent upon wiping out my family, friends, and fellow citizens, how do I reconcile Jesus' teachings about forgiveness; loving our enemies; turning the other cheek; and praying for our persecutors?

- Why do three major religions: Judaism, Islam, and Christianity—all brothers under Abraham—hang onto tribal conflicts instead of embracing one another's Godly roots? (I have encountered Christians in my own culture expressing bigotry toward other faiths, sometimes even toward other Christian denominations!)
- And how in heaven's name can humanity continue to exist without a quantum jump in surrendering to God's love, forgiveness, and guidance in the midst of such aggressive sinfulness and self-centeredness?

On a personal scale, I looked around at people I knew and wondered:

- Why do people so often behave as if they are living on separate planets, with no relationship to one another?
- How do brothers and sisters, parents and children, and other relatives become so angry, abusive, and alienated that they can never speak or even share natural family affection?
- How can men and women belittle, dishonor, and cheat on their spouses, without any awareness about how it will affect their children, family, and friends . . . let alone their own spirits?
- How can we deny the connections of our body, mind, and spirit—disregarding our own physical and mental health with bad habits . . . poisoning our bodies and our minds— yet still expect to live happy and healthy lives?
- If God is indeed trying to communicate with us, why is it so hard for us to hear His messages?

These nagging questions are not signs of lost faith. They are questions we all *must* ask if we hope to heal the suffering in this imperfect world and in ourselves. These questions beg us to find the great bridge between heaven and earth, between our understandings of a spiritual reality and the relentless grind of our worldly lives.

Religion by itself is not the answer; that is certain. In fact, humanity's primitive tendency toward tribal division seems to perpetuate itself through religion. Look at all the religious wars being fought today. Laws and dogmas without God's Spirit tend to divide and seclude. His Spirit, on the other hand, fosters love and empathy toward all people. God wishes us to be *in*clusive, not *ex*clusive. The ugly actions and reactions of religious fanaticism have made it clear that religion, when disconnected from God's guidance, can be terribly misused.

POSTMODERN TWISTS

Ironically, even the concept of unity can be a cause for division between major religious faiths: Many Muslims, embracing the truth that *God is One,* have a difficult time with the Christian belief in a triune God—Father, Son, and Holy Spirit—because it implies that God is not *one* but *three*. And on another boundary, many Christians have difficulty with the Buddhist concept that *All is One,* because it implies that God is everything and therefore doesn't fit with the idea of God as supreme and separate from His fallen creation.

No, I hadn't lost my faith in God. Not at all. In fact, like many people of our day, the events of September 11 served as a wake-up call, which caused me to pray more, to love more sincerely, and to embrace each day as if it were the last. But at the same time, realizing that time is precious, I found myself more confused than ever about *exactly what God wanted me to do with my limited number of days.*

Once again, I considered the questions posed in our show *Miracles, Angels & Afterlife.* Those topics now seemed strangely far away. The here-and-now headlines shouted much louder the more immediate messages of survival.

Years ago, as a young and fanatical Christian, people had warned me against being "too heavenly-minded to be any earthly good." Now, my interest in hearing those purely spiritual stories—which had built a strong and genuine understanding of God's eternal realms—were giving way to a desire to apply those understandings to everyday life.

I felt that my generation had entered a hall of mirrors where even religion is frequently used to disguise selfish ambition—a maze where all possessions, problems, successes, and failures must be reflected in the eternal Spirit of God, in order to decide what is real and permanent.

Personally, I had learned valuable lessons in my pursuits of spiritual experiences. Now, in the face of an even more imperfect world, those truths would be called up from somewhere deep within and tested.

CHAPTER THREE

SPIRITUAL CHALLENGE

*Dear brothers and sisters, whenever trouble comes
your way, let it be an opportunity for joy. For when
your faith is tested, your endurance has a chance to
grow. So let it grow, for when your endurance is
fully developed, you will be strong in character and
ready for anything. If you need wisdom—if you
want to know what God wants you to do—ask
him, and he will gladly tell you. He will not resent
your asking. But when you ask him, be sure that
you really expect him to answer, for a doubtful
mind is as unsettled as a wave of the sea that is
driven and tossed by the wind.*

—James 1:2–6 NLT

Stowe's Journey

Following my mother's death, my immediate family left the Southern charm of Atlanta, Georgia, all of us going our separate ways. Dad moved back to Asheville, North Carolina, where we had lived two years earlier.

Settling in, he began the long process of starting a new life as a widower and single father. My brother Charles began attending the St. Louis School for the Deaf in Missouri, where he would live on and off for the next twelve years.

And I was sent to Glen Ellyn, Illinois, to spend the next eleven months with my father's sister Jane and her husband Tabor.

There could not have been a better place for me to land than in the loving arms of my aunt and uncle and their children. The time spent with their family still stands as one of the highlights of my childhood. It was fortunate for me that my aunt was excited at the prospect of having a little one around the house and didn't mind putting on hold her plans to return to college. She also opted out of putting me into kindergarten so she could spend more time with me. I had many happy times there, and I will always be grateful to her and my cousins for the time they took to nurture my soul.

Being a part of their high-energy family was quite eye opening, and I loved having older "sisters." KD, who was thirteen, and Clare, ten, were thoughtful young ladies who were kind enough to include me in so many of their activities; yet they were also able to get down on my level. I remember searching for birds' nests in the backyard with KD, playing games of hide-and-seek, camping out in their bedroom, and the first time I saw a Chicago snow. Wow! What fun we had. I'll also never forget the night I was first introduced to a relatively new British music group called the Beatles. I can still see us all piled on the den sofa, our eyes glued to the television set. *The Ed Sullivan Show* was about to start, and the excitement in the air generated by my young cousins was intense. Oh, the squealing that went on when the Fab Four started singing and shaking their heads—and I was right in there with them! It's no wonder I've been a Beatles fan all my life.

I hold dear the many memories of my time there, and I

wish I could have stayed longer; but after almost a year my father had secured a job and a house and was ready for me to come home.

Being Mr. Mom in the mid-sixties was not as fashionable as it is these days. My father was definitely of the school where women were supposed to take care of the children. I know it was a heavy burden for him and he did the best he could, considering the circumstances. But even his best intentions were tainted by his alcohol dependence, which he used to cover his pain. Over the years his vision for our well-being was blurred, and though he often meant well, when it came right down to it he seemed, much of the time, to be self-centered and controlling. His loved having parties, and he enjoyed the image of being a playboy.

But despite it all, I loved him dearly. In fact, until I was about fourteen years old, he could do no wrong in my eyes. I closed my ears when people talked about his drinking or called him a tightwad. To me he was strong, fun-loving, and handsome. He was all I had in the world, and when he gave me his full attention I was buoyant.

We lived in a small house in one of the nicer neighborhoods of our little mountain town. All around us were the homes of the well-to-do and inside them lived perfect families. Of course, I now know there is no such thing as the perfect family, but back then I considered our family to be unusually weird. My father was a loud partyer who loved to dress up and drink, my brother was deaf, my mother was dead, and I was a tomboy who did not fit in with other little girls.

I remember once when a girl down the street came to visit. I thought this to be somewhat unusual since I knew she and her sisters didn't like me; but she was friendly enough that day and so I began to warm up to her. We talked as young girls do; a little chitchat. And then she looked at me and said, "My mother told me we had to play with you because you don't have a mother."

I just sat there looking at her, feeling a small crack in my heart open up. I don't remember what I said, but from that moment on I resolved to never let anyone feel sorry for me for not having a mother. I may have been a victim of my circumstances, but I would do my best to be upbeat—in other words, I would hide everything inside. I was too young to know the dangers of this tactic.

My brother was away at school for most of the year, home only on major holidays and during the summer, so most of the time I was the only one my father had to look after. His first attempt at my care was to hire a housekeeper— someone who would live in our home and take care of both of us. It was not an easy job.

My father was a demanding employer, making out long lists of chores. Things had to be done "just so," and although he could afford it, he simply would not pay someone what she was worth. Consequently, over the course of two years, thirty women came and went through our home. Some would stay a few months, others only a few days. Some would try and help put our shattered lives back together. Others would beat me and mentally torture me or worse—just leave me in the middle of the day even as I cried and begged them not to go.

Dad said those two years were very hard on him. I'm sure they were—they certainly were hard for me, though for different reasons. My memory banks are full of unusual experiences, too numerous to list here, brought on by these strange women. There were drunks, Christians, eccentrics, and pure old meanies. They all gave it a shot. Looking back, it's a miracle I'm still alive.

After two years of this torture, Dad finally came to the realization that this kind of child care was just not working out. Perhaps he reasoned it would be better for us to live in someone else's home.

I was six years old when my father put an ad in the newspaper to the effect of, "Two children need a home."

*

Peter

Despite our letdown at the loss of our show *Miracles, Angels & Afterlife,* I realized that my family was not as bad off as others . . . many had lost everything. At least we had our lives and were in good health. Careers come and go, and Stowe and I have always felt that God watches out for us, providing what we need to survive.

But I was undergoing an even deeper test of faith.

A LIGHT GROWING DIM

Here I was, forty-six years old and once again trying to reinvent my career. For thirty-two years I had successfully pursued the life of a filmmaker, following where I felt God was calling. Yes, I had suffered many setbacks, including a ten-year detour that included drugs, alcohol, and a painful first marriage that failed. I had faced my own personal Ground Zero a number of times, and by God's goodness I always returned to Him to light my way.

Still, something was different now. Something had changed.

I don't know if it was simply my age, when my energy to start over again was not what it used to be . . . or if I was just feeling the stress of more responsibility over my young children and our new house mortgage. Whatever the cause, it was unsettling—mainly because *I wasn't sure I still had the calling* to investigate the supernatural topics I had pursued for so long in my television work.

I have always tried to be true to myself and to others, paying attention to my feelings about the correct direction in my life. I believe that one's *creative desire* is a major characteristic of being *"made in God's image"* (Gen. 1:26) as a cocreator and caretaker, or overseer. Also, Jesus' Greatest Commandment has long been my standard for making choices in my life: *"Love the Lord your God with all your heart, with all your soul, with all your mind, and with all your strength . . . Love your neighbor as yourself"* (Mark 12:30–31 HCSB). As a result, I've been led into a creative career path that has been both helpful to other people and rewarding to myself. But now, I felt my "soul, mind and strength" were all growing tired . . . weakened by the relentless juggling act of chasing budgets, racing deadlines, smiling at rejections, and other realities of the TV business—all in order to proclaim a purely spiritual message!

It wasn't that I no longer wanted to help others. It was that I had no burning desire to pursue the same kinds of productions about supernatural phenomena like miracles, angels, and near-death experiences that I had been doing for more than a decade. In fact, I wasn't sure I felt any positive inspirations about doing anything in television or film; nor did I feel the drive one needs to make things happen in that competitive business.

To make my new direction even more puzzling, I also began recognizing my serious misgivings about some of the underpinnings of our civilized society, including inequitable economics, unaffordable health care, vulgarity in media, unhealthy eating habits, rampant materialism, and other distortions of what I consider to be social priorities. In short, I was feeling disconnected from the world around me and from my own purpose in it.

Then, one day, I realized what was happening to me. A part of me was growing slightly bitter, and maybe even angry. Not in a dramatic Jekyll and Hyde sort of way. More like a slow and cumulative vinegar drip, which one day fills up the container and begins to trickle over the top. And I realized that this bitter taste had been building up for a long time—perhaps throughout my life. It was made up of lots of little disappointments, and some big, that I had never completely gotten over. I could feel myself sigh deeply when recalling lost loves and broken friendships. I could feel my fists tighten while thinking back on professional relationships in which I had felt deceived or swindled. And I could see myself turn away from TV evangelists when they reminded me of the terrible discovery, as a young man, that I had been part of a religious cult.

What dawned on me was that the Light in me was growing dimmer. I was slowly, almost imperceptibly, feeling like I was under a collection of gathering clouds, and my life was being overshadowed. And I could tell that these joyless feelings were taking a toll on my physical health. I was feeling pains in my chest and aches in my body, which doctors would only attribute to stress. But I knew there was a cause-and-effect connection between the emotional feelings I was identifying and the physical symptoms I was experiencing. It felt like my body had been storing these bad feelings somewhere out of sight. It seemed like I was harboring a collection of electrical, chemical, and hormonal responses that now were emerging as a bitter aftertaste, taking the edge off my enthusiasm for life.

A DESPERATE PRAYER OF HOPE

I realized, too, that I was sharing a feeling that many others in the world were also experiencing; *a feeling of being damaged by the pains of life . . . isolated, with a sense of separateness.* Little by little, I was losing awareness of my personal connections with God and with those around me. I had simply become unconscious of God's Spirit in my life.

Perhaps Osama bin Laden had served as the trigger, I don't know; but I now felt the cumulative effects of a lifetime of disappointments in religious fanaticism, political hatreds, and other forms of intolerance. And I also knew that if I didn't deal with my own personal feelings of smoldering resentment, I could one day become a victim of their destructive effects. I didn't want my subconscious negative chants of "I'm sick and tired of ——" or "That just makes me ill" to unwittingly manifest themselves as sickness and fatigue in my physical life.

Deep in my heart, a prayer began to emerge:

Lord, I may not know exactly where these feelings of frustration, fear, and resentment came from; but I begin to feel them hanging over me like a dark cloud, blocking me from Your life-giving Light. And I know that You can heal anyone of anything. Please deal with my heart, and let me rise above these clouds so I can find my way into Your Light again. Amen.

This prayer began a new leg of my ongoing journey, to strive to be closer to God, to live in His will, and reconnect to that part of myself that links directly to Him in *Spirit*—the Spirit He breathed into all of us at our creation.

Stowe

I read the words Peter wrote, and I felt a little wisp of sadness fall upon my heart. I realized that underneath his usually solid and upbeat character, Peter was someone who—just like all of us at times—was hurting somewhere deep inside. And despite his strong faith, he was beginning to feel cut off from the Light and love of God.

My husband's troubled frame of mind is a familiar feeling to many people in today's world. Sudden changes in direction, whether by layoff, divorce, death of a loved one, or any number of unforeseen events, can leave us feeling resentful, frustrated, and bitter. We discover ourselves feeling disconnected from our own sense of purpose in life, which can lead to a sense of alienation from others.

For many, this downward spiral may continue when the routine stress is no longer vented in the old familiar ways, which leads to a buildup of adrenaline. Add to that a lack of exercise, unhealthy eating habits, alcohol or drugs (even prescription drugs), and we can find our bodies laden with toxins. Some of the distressing consequences to this kind of living are pain, fatigue, and poor health, not to mention depression and confusion.

After all is said and done, we may feel as though we have been wandering aimlessly through a confusing maze only to wind up on a dead-end path, sorely in need of physical or emotional healing. We're trapped inside the shell of our ego, and the worst part is that we often don't even realize it. In our desperate fight to maintain our independent and self-respecting egos, we may cut ourselves off from everything and everyone, including the healing love of God.

As a wife, it was hard to see my husband going through the difficult down times of his own life's journey. I wanted to help him in some way because I know what it's like to feel disconnected. For me, the slow drip began when my mother died; and it began to pour like a broken faucet the day my father told the world, "Two children need a home." I knew I had no real power to start Peter's healing. Sure, I could encourage him and pray for his healing; but it was his own prayer, his own faith, that could finally lead to his healing and his return to God's Light.

> *Find rest, O my soul, in God alone; my hope comes from him. He alone is my rock and my salvation; he is my fortress, I will not be shaken. My salvation and my honor depend on God; he is my might, my refuge. Trust in him at all times, O people; pour out your hearts to him, for God is our refuge.*
>
> —PSALMS 62:5–8 NIV

CHAPTER FOUR

THE SEPARATED SELF

*I do not understand what I do. For what I want to
do I do not do, but what I hate I do. . . . For I have
the desire to do what is good, but I cannot carry it
out. For what I do . . . the evil I do not want to
do—this I keep on doing. . . . What a wretched
man I am! Who will rescue me from this
body of death?*

—ROM. 7:15, 18–19, 24 NIV

Stowe's Journey

The Turner family answered the ad. They lived only a few miles down the road from us, and it was decided that I would stay there through the week and spend some weekends with my dad. My brother would stay there whenever he was in town.

The Turner family consisted of Lucky, Martha, and their daughter Cynthia. I have no idea why they chose to keep me and, occasionally, my brother. I suppose they did it for the money, though it couldn't have been much. Martha was a tall woman in her thirties with a snowy white beehive hairdo who, on Sunday nights when my father brought me to their house, smiled and patted my head gently, only to begin hissing and swatting at me the minute he left.

Lucky, who was a little shorter than his wife, wore a

crew cut and thick black glasses. I remember his tobacco-stained, widely spaced teeth, which made him look rather unattractive. He smoked nonfiltered Lucky Strike cigarettes and was someone who could often be found in a dark and dingy roadside tavern. (I know this because he sometimes took me with him. I was usually told I couldn't stay inside and so spent the remainder of the time alone in the car.)

During the time I lived with the Turners, Lucky worked either as a truck driver for the Schlitz Beer Company or as a house painter. Martha was a stay-at-home mother, and their daughter Cynthia was an angry and rebellious fourteen-year-old who did not appreciate having another little girl around the house. They also took in for a time a sad little red-haired boy named David, whom I never really got to know. Also living in the house was Martha's mother, a crabby old woman with a walker who dipped snuff and barked at little children. The Turners drove a black 1965 Fairlane and lived in a yellow stucco house beside a busy highway.

I stayed with them for two years.

Everyone who knew me as a child remembers me as a cheerful, easygoing little girl. I liked to please people. But there was no pleasing the Turners, and during the time I lived there I became a little girl filled with shame. It seemed to me that everything I did was wrong. Constantly accused of breaking things or going against their wishes, I began to withdraw into my own world, separating myself from everyone around me.

Much of my free time was spent up in an apple tree, whispering to the birds and staring at the blue sky. It was so beautiful up there. *Why couldn't I just fly away like the birds?* But I was trapped and alone. I seemed to be living in a world where I was unwanted—where no one loved me. Even so, I tried not to dwell on these thoughts for too long. I made excuses for my father's behavior as well as the Turners'. I was not one to feel sorry for myself, and so, trying to make others laugh seemed to be the best way around the pain.

I'm not sure how long I had been living there, six months or so, when I was startled awake one night by a hand groping me under the covers; touching me in places I hardly knew existed. I sat up in bed, scared, searching the darkness for a clue as to who was there. I looked toward Cynthia who was sleeping beside me. Just then a hand went over my mouth and pushed me back down toward my pillow. As my eyes adjusted to the dim light, I looked up and began to make out the face. In a hushed voice Lucky told me to be quiet and lie still. He was smiling, and I could almost see him winking at me in the dark. He put his lips close to my ear and told me this would be our little secret.

It was a horrible secret that I would keep buried for the next thirteen years.

There were other encounters with Lucky during my stay there, but somehow I had the feeling Martha was suspicious of him, so he and I were not allowed too much time alone together. But the seeds of sexuality had been planted in me, and they would be tended frequently over the next few years.

It wasn't just Lucky, though, who exposed me to the darkness of sexual abuse. Once, when Cynthia had a date, her mother said she would have to take me along. Cynthia was furious about this, and after riding a few miles down the road, they stopped the car and ordered me into the trunk. Later that night at a drive-in movie, they took me out and let me sit in the backseat. I remember the salty taste of boxed popcorn as I watched my first porno movie while Cynthia and her boyfriend made out in the front seat.

I was only six years old.

My father picked me up for weekends—I was always so happy to see him. He fetched me on Friday afternoons and sometimes we went out to eat with one of his girlfriends and her children. During the summer when my brother was home we almost seemed like a real family. We had some good times despite Dad's love of Scotch (he always managed to sneak it into restaurants), and fortunately one of his girlfriends was always there to drive us home.

Saturdays were usually spent doing errands and going out to lunch, while in the evening I often helped Dad prepare for parties or dates. I loved our times together. Under his careful guidance I happily learned how to iron his clothes and shine his shoes. He was a spiffy dresser, and it was fun watching him get ready for his dates. I usually spent the rest of the evening watching TV.

No matter how late he stayed out on Saturday night, we always went to church on Sunday. Dad loved participating in the doctrine and rituals of the Episcopal Church. Dressing in our Sunday best was a must. I never really understood all the fuss—his life the other six days of the week did not strike me as a very spiritual existence; but perhaps it had something to do with his upbringing. He wanted to do the right thing—the things his parents had taught him to do. Anyway, Sunday afternoons were usually spent hanging out or visiting with his friends, and then it was the dreaded evening drive back to the Turners.

During my stay with the Turners I went through first

and second grades. Because I was a very thin child, I became the brunt of many "skinny" jokes. I felt like a social outcast, and I was shy and awkward with my peers. I found comfort on the sidelines of the playground, playing with rocks and staring at clouds. I was an average student in all subjects, except by second grade I was failing math. Because of this I was required to stay after school for tutoring by my teacher, Mrs. Hall. She was a wonderful young lady who, looking back, probably understood me more than I knew. She was warm and gentle—I sometimes wished she would be my mother. Yet even with her kindness, it was degrading to stay after school all by myself, and I began to have the feeling that everyone in the world was smarter than me.

Peter

It's very simple: Without God's love—or rather, the *knowledge* of God's love—our lives feel meaningless and empty. I have heard it said that within each one of us is a God-shaped hole—an empty place only our Creator can fill. But unfortunately we are often blind to this. We ignore it, or we don't recognize it.

THE SEPARATED SELF

Led by our bruised egos or circumstances beyond our control, we frequently find ourselves bumping around in the darkness trying even harder to connect to something that will either give us a feeling of self worth, or else we try to find some way to medicate the pain. I call this condition the *separated self*.

The *separated self*:

- is unaware of the connection between itself and its Creator.
- is unaware of the interreliance of its own parts—body, mind, and spirit.
- is unconscious of its spiritual connections with other people.
- often just can't remember where to begin reconnecting.

And here is the strange thing: This isn't a tragic anomaly shared only by children whose fates are controlled by ungodly adults. Even people whose long journey has offered many spiritual insights can still find themselves caught in a separated state now and again. It is just part of our human nature.

One of life's little occurrences recently spoke to me about healing one facet of the separated self. As it turned out, this story was more than just an amusing anecdote—I found meaning in it and interpreted it to fit my own circumstances at that time.

REFLECTIONS OF THE WORLD

I was helping our neighbors, the Williamses, move some furniture into their new house. Our dog Belle had been shadowing me, poking around in their garage where we had just unloaded some pieces of beds, dressers, and the like. As I passed through the garage, I saw a startling scene: Belle had turned a corner and was standing face-to-face with a dog she had never seen. She instantly froze in her tracks, and the other dog did the same. Belle took on the stance dogs do when they are ready to defend their turf. The new dog responded in kind. Belle, who is normally very sweet with other animals, was not at all comfortable with this unusually defensive rival. Her lip curled on one side, baring her teeth as a message of her supremacy; but the other dog didn't cower. Instead it returned the snarl, which caused Belle to ratchet up her threat to a full-faced show of fangs, making her look more like a wolf than I ever thought possible. The other dog became equally terrifying, and soon the low growling had descended into deep and spine-tingling primal canine sounds heard in the wilds around carcasses of freshly killed prey. Belle, I have to say, had met her match, and the next moment promised a bloody confrontation between two fearful and enraged enemies.

The only thing that kept the scene from exploding into a grisly collision was the sound of laughter, erupting from all of us humans standing around watching this prehistoric, territorial drama as it unfolded. Before Belle could charge at her ferocious adversary, I managed to slide in beside her, soothing her with a calm voice and a reassuring pat on the head. She stayed locked to the eyes of the other dog, watching in puzzlement as a strangely familiar person slid down to restrain her opponent. She looked up at me, and then back at the other dog, and then back to me again.

"Belle," I whispered, "its okay, girl. You're safe." Over our hysterical laughter, I continued, "Belle . . . it's a mirror! That dog you're getting so mad at . . . is you!" I led her up to the bedroom mirror, which was leaning against the wall, and tapped on the reflection of my own hand. It dawned on me that Belle, being an outdoor dog, had never seen a mirror and therefore didn't recognize her own image. After a few bewildered moments of dealing with this strange new magic, Belle made friends with the mirror dog, and they eventually went their separate ways.

So often, when we see things in other people we don't like or that make us uncomfortable or afraid, aren't we really seeing something about ourselves that we're struggling with? It's the same with personalities we enjoy—when someone smiles at us, we can't help but smile back. Humans are so connected and so alike. In fact, with our deep spiritual roots, people in our lives often act like mirrors. They can teach us a lot about ourselves.

Stowe

I know exactly what Peter means about looking at other people as reflections of ourselves. If we look closely, we may see fear, rejection, and pain. But we may also see a mirror of God's Light, the love that Christ embodied. God's Light, through whom all things were made, is traveling through His creation, which includes us. In order for God's Light to fulfill its journey, we must willingly allow the healing of our separated self, fixing our spiritual connections so we can know the unity we share with God and with each other.

But a seed must fall to the ground and die before it can grow; and that means we often must look closely into the eyes of our fellow humans and see a reflection of the fallen nature of man—separated and self-serving.

CHAPTER FIVE

OUR FALLEN NATURE

*For the flesh sets its desire against the Spirit, and
the Spirit against the flesh; for these are in
opposition to one another, so that you may not do
the things that you please.*

—GAL. 5:17 NASB

Stowe's Journey

Turning seven is a big event for any child, and so for my seventh birthday my father promised me a big party. He bought me a number seven candle with a little monkey on it.

I eagerly awaited the big day, dreaming of the cake with that special candle . . . but for reasons unknown to me, that party never took place. I was crushed. And so, to make it up to me, my eighth birthday was more of a party. I received quite a few presents, too, and they were all brought to the Turners' house. But as soon as Dad left, Mrs. Turner took my gifts and locked them up in a closet in the garage. "I don't want a bunch of toys in my house," she seethed.

My tears meant nothing to her. I'll never forget seeing that big brown door close on my toys. I never saw them again, and it was years before I told my father about it.

It occurs to me, as I now write this, why I have never liked birthdays. I always feel uncomfortable on "the day."

By the spring of 1969, communication between my father and the Turners had become quite heated. They were constantly accusing my brother and me of breaking things and then trying to get my father to pay for them. I never heard anything nice said about my father or me, and it was difficult to defend myself in the face of all the accusations. I'm not sure how it all came to a head as far as me leaving the Turners' house, but I am sure it had something to do with my final encounter with Lucky.

It started one afternoon when Lucky and I were home alone. I was in his and Martha's bedroom, looking at some things on their dresser that actually belonged to me. I discovered they had my silver teething ring and baby cup. I was happy to see these little treasures again, and I couldn't help but wonder, *Why are these things here?* That's when Lucky came in. Taking my hand, he led me over to the bed. Smiling, he pulled his pants down and sat on the edge of the bed. I remember staring at his private parts as he pulled my own pants down. I wasn't sure what was happening but I felt scared; something seemed different from our other encounters. He pulled me closer to him and asked me to touch him. At that moment we heard the sound of tires pulling in the gravel drive. He quickly threw me off of him and ordered me to dress while he frantically pulled at his pants. His face was flushed and his voice strained as he pushed me out of the room and told me to go to my bedroom to play. "Don't say anything!" he commanded.

I was barely out of their bedroom when the front door flew open. I froze and looked downstairs to see Martha coming in with a grocery bag in each arm. She took one look at me from the bottom of the steps and, throwing her bags down, began climbing the stairs. She was mad. "What have you been doing?" she hissed.

I glanced over at Lucky, who was still sitting on the bed and waving his hands at me. I looked back at her. "Nothing," I said softly.

"You're lying," she said through gritted teeth. Reaching the top of the steps, she pushed me aside and yelled, "Get out of here!"

I saw the bedroom door slam shut, and then the screaming began. I went to my room, completely unaware of the fact that the good Lord had just rescued me from a child's worst nightmare.

I don't remember anything about the Turners after that. Perhaps I left immediately—I don't know. I do know my father had a lot of trouble getting some of our personal belongings back, and the Turners, of course, said he owed them money.

After a while, though, things settled down. I was glad to be home, and Dad was glad to have us out of there and away from those horrible people. Oh, if he had only known. . . .

It was over thirty years later that I told my father about some of the things the Turners did to me—even then, I just couldn't tell it *all*.

I suppose I thought that, even in light of my father's own fallen nature, the truth would be too much for him . . . or maybe I had simply grown too accustomed to locking everything inside. Even as an adult I didn't recognize my own fallen nature and how I had become so hopelessly disconnected from God.

*

Jesus answered, "Truly, truly, I say to you, unless
one is born of water and the Spirit he cannot enter
into the kingdom of God. That which is born of the
flesh is flesh, and that which is born of the Spirit is
spirit. Do not be amazed that I said to you, 'You
must be born again.' The wind blows where it
wishes and you hear the sound of it, but do not
know where it comes from and where it is going; so
is everyone who is born of the Spirit."

—JOHN 3:5–8 NASB

Peter

The first and worst disconnection in need of healing, before any other, is the separation between God and us. This split between our egos—our mind, our consciousness, or whatever we normally think of as *self*—and the Spirit of God is that great division often called our *fallen nature*. This is what some people think of as Adam and Eve's original sin—or turning away from God. Unfortunately, our pride can prevent us from taking the first step toward healing that separation; yet it is a reconnection that can be initiated only by us, individually, through an act of faith.

Our spirit is our true self. It is the spark, the very essence of life that God breathed into humankind. The original Hebrew and Aramaic words for spirit were respectively *ruwach* and *pneuma,* which meant breath or wind. Gen. 1:2 reads, *"The Spirit* [Breath] *of God was hovering over the face of the waters"* (NKJV; emphasis mine). And Gen. 2:7 says, *"The LORD God formed man of the dust of the ground, and breathed into his nostrils the breath of life* [Spirit], *and man became a living being"* (NKJV; emphasis mine).

When I die and cease breathing, it is because the Spirit—

the breath of life—leaves my body. The problem with my day-to-day life is that I have forgotten that *I am Spirit*. I have come to believe that I am really Peter Shockey . . . a male human being . . . college educated . . . a writer and producer of books and TV shows . . . the husband of Stowe Shockey . . . father of Christina and Grace Shockey . . . currently attending a Presbyterian church . . . living in the twenty-first century . . . in the Southeastern United States, etc. But that is *not really* who I am—at least not originally. I am a gust of Spirit. I am only here on earth and able to perceive life because I am a breath of God . . . one exhale of the Creator. And I will be inhaled again, relatively soon. This is true for us all. We are vessels of God's breath and wouldn't be here otherwise. Yet we have all forgotten—or blocked out, or whatever term best describes the *fallen state* of humanity—our conscious connection to God through the Spirit.

BUYING INTO THE LIE

Again, original sin—as portrayed in the Genesis story—was Adam and Eve's *buying into the belief* that they could sneak around unseen, separate, and disconnected. And we all seem to have inherited that curse, living as if we were disconnected from our source and from one another. Cheating—whether on one's spouse, diet, tests, or taxes—is just one example of self-deception that says, *This is okay, as long as I keep it hidden.* But two problems result: The first is that nothing can be hidden forever—sooner or later the truth catches up with us; and the second is that, sadly, whenever we enforce the idea that we can hide our thoughts and actions, we further cut off our life-giving connections.

I am firmly convinced of this: The commonly accepted belief that we are all separate entities, veiled and disconnected, is the root of all human sin and suffering; and this is the very reason we find ourselves cut off from the miraculous life and power that Jesus promised we would inherit when He said:

> *Have faith in me when I say that the Father is one*
> *with me and that I am one with the Father. Or else*
> *have faith in me simply because of the things I do. I*
> *tell you for certain that if you have faith in me, you*
> *will do the same things that I am doing. You will*
> *do even greater things, now that I am going back to*
> *the Father. Ask me, and I will do whatever you ask.*
> *This way the Son will bring honor to the Father. I*
> *will do whatever you ask me to do.*
>
> —JOHN 14:11–14 CEV

Here's a metaphor to help you consider spiritual disconnection in terms of sickness: A debate exists between medical doctors and so-called holistic practitioners in regard to the treatment of a disease—say cancer, for example. A medical doctor may prescribe a combination of surgery, chemotherapy, and radiation as treatment for eliminating the cancerous tumor. A holistic practitioner, on the other hand, may argue that such treatments deal only with the symptom—a tumor—and in order to cure the patient, one must also deal with the underlying conditions that made the patient vulnerable to cancer in the first place.

Now compare spiritual disconnection with disease. If I complain about being disconnected from other people—from society, from my purpose in life, or even from my own feelings—am I not simply identifying symptoms of a bigger underlying problem? Could it be I am suffering from a disconnection from God—my source—and have become vulnerable to the collapse of my relationships with everything and everyone else?

I have always had a problem with the basic idea of *sin,* which many people treat like a tumor. They may use the word *sin* to describe assorted activities like smoking, drinking, adultery, murder . . . even eating chocolate. But are those things actually the sin, or are they the *symptoms* of original sin?

One of the definitions for the ancient Greek word for sin is *to miss the mark,* like when an archer's arrow misses its target. Sin in my life—missing the target—is the condition of not enjoying the wholeness of life God designed for me. So I can battle individual sins all my life, but the real problem is, if God's Spirit does not guide me, I'm like an archer wearing a blindfold.

THE GREATEST COMMANDMENT

What is the real target, then, if I wasn't missing it? In a perfect world—if I were indeed connected with God and always knew His will for my life—what mark would I be hitting? What is my purpose as a human? If avoiding specific sins isn't the whole purpose in life, then what is?

Jesus once answered a tricky question, *"Teacher, which is the greatest commandment in the law?"* (Matt. 22:36 NIV). Obsessed with do's and don'ts, the Pharisee was probably trying to ask, "What is the most important sin to avoid?" Jesus replied:

"Love the Lord your God with all your heart and with all your soul and with all your mind." This is the first and greatest commandment. And the second is like it: "Love your neighbor as yourself." All the Law and the Prophets hang on these two commandments.

(MATT. 22:37–40 NIV)

Love. Love. Love. Love God. Love your neighbor. Love yourself. This is the meaning of life. This is the bull's-eye of the target. But, speaking for myself, I was born with lousy aim. Some part of me has trouble believing in *original sin*. Perhaps I've had difficulty believing that God would punish us all for an ancestral bite of an apple . . . a hard idea to swallow. However it all got started, I can't deny that humanity seems to be bred with a built-in tendency to make stupid and selfish decisions. I see it in myself, I see it in extremely young children, and I see it every time I read the newspaper. We all regularly and predictably miss the mark. So what is our sinful nature?

- To not love God.
- To not love others.
- To not treat even ourselves with love.
- To be self-centered, which has nothing to do with love of any kind.

So, regardless of whether this so-called fallen nature is some kind of punishment or something we just fell into, it is a condition we still must face. And yet here is the puzzling thing: Alongside our nature to do wrong, I can also find evidence of God's Spirit in people. It is sometimes called the *still small voice*. Cartoons characterize this voice as the angelic advocate on one shoulder, whispering in one ear to reject the devil's advice in our other ear; it is the part of us that really desires to do the right thing. It speaks to us, and we decide to listen or not—mostly not. But we continually face the fork in the road, deciding to either follow the guidance of God's Spirit or follow the desires of our lower nature. And each time we choose the low road rather than the Spirit, we find ourselves a little farther away and a little more disconnected from our source. The good news is that by first recognizing these two sides of ourselves, we can then at least make an informed decision.

MADE FOR COMMUNITY

As a young man, I found it extremely meaningful to discover that, although life seemed to be an endless struggle between these two sides, I was originally created by the Light of God. John's Gospel introduces the Light of Christ by saying:

> *In the beginning the Word already existed. He was*
> *with God, and he was God. He was in the begin-*
> *ning with God. He created everything there is.*
> *Nothing exists that he didn't make. Life itself was*
> *in him, and this life gives light to everyone. The*
> *light shines through the darkness, and the darkness*
> *can never extinguish it.*
> —JOHN 1:1–5 NLT

From my own experiences and those of others I have known, I am reassured on an almost daily basis that we were created in this Light. We were not meant to be separate, neither from God nor from each other. We were created in God's image (Gen. 1:27).

To rediscover our true selves, as children of the Light (John 1:10–13), we must return to a relationship with the Spirit of God. It's a lifelong journey, to remain as connected as possible. The one sure way to heal our various disconnected relationships is to regularly and willingly return to our spiritual source . . . the Light of God. Of course, it isn't as simple as it sounds; and most of us must walk through miles of treacherous and dark territory before we arrive at the source of our Light. Sadly, some of us even have to go through a vast wilderness period where we are convinced we are completely alone in the world and entirely abandoned by God.

CHAPTER SIX

ABANDONED AND ALONE

*Take heed that you do not despise one of these little
ones, for I say to you that in heaven their angels
always see the face of My Father who is in
heaven. . . . If a man has a hundred sheep, and one
of them goes astray, does he not leave the ninety-
nine and go to the mountains to seek the one that is
straying? . . . Even so it is not the will of your
Father who is in heaven that one of these little ones
should perish.*

—MATT. 18:10, 12, 14 NKJV

Stowe's Journey

The summer of 1969 began on a high note—a trip to
Six Flags Over Georgia and some fun picnics and
backyard adventures. And then one day my father
came to me and said he was taking my brother and me to
live on a beautiful farm in the mountains. "You'll love it,"
he said as he described the place. "You'll be staying with
a family called Grey. There'll be other children there, and
Mrs. Grey says they even have a horse you can ride."

It sounded okay. So we loaded up our pale yellow Fairlane 500 and rode about an hour and a half out of town into
rural country before turning onto a long and winding driveway. At the end, perched upon a hill and surrounded by

mountains, stood a large gray farmhouse with a trailer sitting to one side. The once white paint of the old house had long since peeled off the clapboard, giving it a dark and somewhat dismal look. I thought, *Surely this has to be the wrong place.*

Mrs. Grey came out to greet us in the driveway. She had a weathered face and, looking back, I think she was probably much younger than she looked—maybe late thirties. Her dress was plain cotton and, like the rest of her, seemed to be worn thin from years of use. But she managed a quiet smile and gave us a little tour of the grounds. I remember her taking me to a pasture and pointing to an old horse they had. She promised to let me ride it someday soon.

And then my father said it was time for him to go. For the first time in my life I felt scared—scared that I would never see my father again. I knew Charles felt the same way, too. As Dad hugged us good-bye, we begged him not to leave us there. He smiled and patted my head. "Don't worry," he said. "Just have fun." Then he turned and walked away.

My brother and I sat on the front steps of the Greys' house, holding onto one another, shaking and crying, watching helplessly as our father left us. All our cries for him to come back were swallowed up in a cloud of dust as his car disappeared around the bend of the dirt road. I felt sure that he was never coming back.

We had been abandoned.

Mrs. Grey left us to cry, but after a while she reappeared and told us to come into the house and have a look around. With swollen eyes, we solemnly followed her. Once inside the house, I saw the dirty, sad faces of children. They were everywhere. One room she showed us had row after row of cribs filled with crying babies. Sad-eyed girls and boys sat quietly on the old stairway.

I didn't like it in the big house and, fortunately for us, there was no room for us to sleep there, so we were given a room in the trailer next door. I suppose it was some relatives of the Greys who lived there, but I never got to know them. After all, we only slept there. The rest of the time we were either working in the fields picking weeds or hanging around on the porch.

Children were beaten regularly for talking, making noise, or general disobedience. I guess Charles and I were two of the lucky ones. Perhaps it was because we were new, but even though we were sometimes hit (I believe unjustly), I think they treated us a little better than some of the other kids.

There was one thing, however, for which I was punished daily—eating, or maybe I should say not eating. As a child I was always a finicky eater—I have miles of memories of all kinds of women forcing me to eat—and it was no different at the Greys; except that her food, which included sour-tasting goat's milk, was the worst I ever had. Always the last one at the table, I was brought into the kitchen so she could watch me while she cleaned the dishes. There was a large slop bucket in the corner that was used to dump garbage to feed the pigs. My objective was to dump my food there without getting caught—but I was rarely successful. The rest of the time I caught the woman's wrath on my backside.

The first time my father called to say hello, I was taken firmly by the arm into the foyer where the old 1920s-style telephone was located and told in no uncertain terms that there would be hell to pay if I told my father anything other than we were fine. I agreed and was lifted up to the phone.

They held the receiver to my ear, and I melted at the sound of my father's voice—he had not forgotten us!

It was a short conversation. I remember him asking if we were having fun. I told him we were—everything was okay. Afterward Mrs. Grey patted my back and said, "You done good."

The next time I heard from my father he was calling from Charlotte, North Carolina, to say he was coming to get us. If being left there was the saddest day of my life, then hearing those words made that day surely the happiest. Charles and I jumped up and down on our beds, hugging each other and crying tears of joy.

I would learn years later the reason for Dad's sudden retrieval of his children. He had gone to Charlotte to visit a friend. After telling her where we were, he said her mouth dropped open. "Dick!" she exclaimed. "Those people were once jailed for child abuse. I read about them in the paper. You've got to get them out of there!" He called us immediately.

A year or so after our departure, we heard the Greys had been arrested again for child abuse.

Looking back, I am just amazed at how God uses people to help one another. I can't help but believe my father's friend in Charlotte had been sent by one of God's heroic angels to warn him of our danger. And once again, I feel blessed to have been plucked out of a bad situation that could have been much worse if we'd stayed there much longer.

Admittedly, those were dark days for me. Back then it often felt as if no one cared for me, much less cared to rescue me. But fortunately, those feelings have passed. They have been replaced with a deep gratitude for my Creator's love for me and awe for how He accomplishes His works. True, I don't always understand everything He does; but in my heart I rest assured that He is in charge.

✴

[Jesus said] In them is fulfilled the prophecy of Isaiah: "You will be ever hearing but never understanding; you will be ever seeing but never perceiving. For this people's heart has become calloused; they hardly hear with their ears, and they have closed their eyes. Otherwise they might see with their eyes, hear with their ears, understand with their hearts and turn, and I would heal them."

—MATT. 13:14–15 NIV

Peter

Earlier I discussed *original sin*, or humanity's *fallen nature*. Now, in light of following Stowe's journey, I want to suggest a rather simple consideration: In the beginning, before the event that some call humanity's fall from grace, I believe we were designed to be fully conscious of God and His Spirit within us. In fact, I think we were just as aware of Him and our relationship with Him as we are currently aware of the physical universe around us—an obvious and undeniable reality.

But something happened that made us unconscious of God and his Spirit. Something caused us to forget or, maybe more accurately, to lose our *sense* of spirit, and thus we became unconscious of God. Some say it happened overnight, while other theorists believe it was the cumulative effect of generations of selfish choices. No matter how one interprets the story of *the fall*, it is obvious to me, as a member of the human species, that I was not born and bred with a conscious awareness of God's Spirit in me.

I also know that at a specific moment in my own life—when I accepted Christ's offer to manifest Himself in my heart—I *suddenly became* acutely aware of a whole new spiritual dimension within me. I believe it was what Jesus called *being born of the Spirit.*

From that moment forward, I understood what it meant to "have ears to hear" and "eyes to see," as Jesus spoke about in Matthew 13. I realized I was not alone.

No, I certainly don't hear or see the Lord's direction in my life on a day-to-day basis. Actually, most of the time I am painfully out of touch with this kind of direct contact, which I have experienced only a few memorable times since my initial encounter. But the fact that I have consciously experienced His living Spirit at all—even if it had happened only once—is enough proof for me to have become a follower of Jesus for my entire lifetime . . . the awareness was just that powerful.

Admittedly, I am not free from original sin, and I struggle every day with that feeling of separation from God—and from other people. And although I long for a loud and clear signal from God, to be able to see and hear Him as I believe humans were originally designed to do, I am still at a point where I have to try awfully hard! I strain to hear, squint to see, and lean in to understand what still seems like a dim signal.

But when I do try to follow the directions I get, even though the directions may be subtle, I find that my life is guided toward the greatest good—for me, my family, and those in my circle of influence. One undeniable result of all this *trying* is that my faith in God's guidance is constantly strengthened. Banished is my fear that I have been forsaken to struggle alone through the dark places of this life.

PART II
SEARCHLIGHTS
OF HOPE

CHAPTER SEVEN

A LIGHT IN THE
DARKNESS

*"Whoever receives one such child in my name
receives me."*

—MATT. 18:5 ESV

Stowe's Journey

"Two Children Need a Home . . ."

Judy McDonald loved to read the want ads. Puppies, sofas, bicycles for sale, jobs wanted—she never knew what she might find. But she was haunted by the ad about two children needing a home. She had seen it in the paper every day for two weeks, and it was almost Christmas, 1969. She worried about these two children whom she assumed had no home. Finally, after consulting with her husband, she called my father and they arranged a time for a visit.

It was a Saturday morning when Dad approached me and asked if I would like to go and stay with a family out in the country—just for a few hours. *Uh oh, here we go again*, I thought. But upon arriving at the house, I was greeted warmly by a beautiful young lady named Judy,

along with her daughter and two sons. We hit it off immediately.

After a few hours, Dad came back to get me, and we
went home and had a little talk. "How did you like staying at the McDonalds' house today?" he asked.

"Oh, I had great time," I said.

"Do you think you would like to live with them?" he
asked, smiling hopefully.

"Yes," I screamed, jumping up and down and clapping
my hands. I couldn't believe my good fortune. Later in life
I would recall how, for the first time, I was able to make a
decision about who my caretakers were. It turns out I made
a pretty wise choice.

So, just a few days before Christmas and with about a
foot of snow on the ground, my father and I headed out to
the country to my dream home. The long dirt driveway,
which led back to the McDonald's little house in the
woods, was covered with snow too deep to traverse by car,
so Judy met us out at the road.

I'll never forget that happy moment.

After unloading my sled from the car and putting my
little suitcase on it, I hugged my father good-bye. Then,
holding Judy's hand, we walked through the snowy won-
derland back to her little house, pulling the sled with my
belongings on the back.

It was one of the best Christmases of my life. I had finally found a home.

The McDonalds loved me and I loved them. For the first
time I was really able to experience the dynamics of a real
family. I had a new sister, Lynee, and two new brothers,
Joey and Jamie. Judy's husband Joe was an airplane pilot,

and even though he was gone quite a bit, he managed to play an important role in my still-formative development.

My father did not pay them much for keeping me, a mere twenty-three dollars a week; but even so, the McDonalds gave me everything they had. It was a genuine love—a love I desperately needed to believe existed in the world.

In this family I was technically the oldest; Joey was only six months younger, so for the first time in my life I assumed a leadership role—and my confidence grew. With the great outdoors to explore, my creative spirit soared. We built roads and forts in the woods, we searched for gold and fossils, and we raised puppies and kittens. We worked, too. And even though it was not my favorite thing to do, I did, in the end, gain a lot of satisfaction from it.

God had provided for me exactly what I needed—a good pot to grow in and establish some roots. I still cherish the many happy memories of carefree hours spent playing in cow fields and woods and walking country roads. It was a wonderful way to grow up, and it is why Peter and I would choose, many years later, to raise our girls in the country.

By the end of 1970 I was spending fewer weekends with my father, and this was probably just as well—his party life had really heated up. I remember more and more parties during this time and scary rides home on Sunday evenings with Dad at the wheel and the car swerving on and off the road. I was always glad to fall back into the safe and loving arms of Judy.

My stay at the McDonalds' house made me feel special for the first time in nine years of life. *Could it be that I am not destined to be a hopeless victim forever?* I had every reason to wonder why, suddenly, something good was happening to me.

✳

Peter

In my line of work as a writer and television producer, I have heard hundreds of stories of miraculous healings and other divine interventions, and I have to admit they can be very uplifting . . . for some. Others may find that these stories cause them to doubt the strength of their faith, or they may be skeptical about the rosy pictures they imply.

WHY SOME AND NOT OTHERS?

One evening, while I was showing our film *Life After Life* to a gathering at the Washington Home and Hospice, a woman raised an unanswerable question: "Why do you think amazing things happen to some people, but not others?" She had such a pained expression, I realized she must have a personal reason for asking, so I awkwardly tried to deal with the complex question I really could not answer. After the meeting, she told me her story.

Five years earlier, the woman was rock-climbing with her husband when he lost his footing and fell to his death. She was left with her three children and the haunting question: *Why?* She tried to satisfy her longing to know: *Where was God? Where were the rescuing angels when her husband fell?* The part of our film that troubled her most, though, dealt with people who returned from their close call with death. These near-death survivors often say that, although they didn't want to return to their bodies and would have preferred to stay in the presence of the glorious Light, they felt compelled to come back because of the strong love they had for their family—a spouse who couldn't live without them or children who needed raising. The woman's grief was etched on her face and her tears glistened as she insisted, "But I know Tom loved us, so why didn't he return?"

I tried to reason, explaining that, in most reported cases, a person was able to return only if the body was capable of being revived. In the case of severe head trauma, there probably was no such choice. She may have heard me . . . I don't know.

Since that time I have known many people who have heard stories about miracles, angels, divine interventions, and near-death experiences, and are left only with the lamenting question: "Why do miraculous things happen to some people and not others?" The flip side of that question is: "Why do terrible things happen to good people?"

In both cases I believe the unspoken question may really be: "Doesn't God love me, too?"

In Hindu culture there is an implication that a person's suffering is punishment from God. The doctrine of karma suggests that a person's afflictions are paybacks for misdeeds, committed either in this life or a previous one. As a result, one who suffers from illness and misfortune is frequently shunned by family and friends. This perception of God as being judgmental and changeable—capable of mood swings and revenge—is comparable to the one-sided view of hell and judgment that some Christians seem to focus on. I find both of these religious views inconsistent with the loving and forgiving God that Jesus describes for us.

A capricious god—one who declares love on one day and

condemns on the next—is not the God I know and grew to love. I firmly believe, without any doubt, in God's eternal and unconditional love for every one of his children.

But the mystery "Why some and not others?" is as complicated as life itself. There are no simple answers, and nowadays my first reply is usually, "I really don't know how to answer that." So, when faced with this question by someone who truly can't comprehend the answer, I say a silent prayer for God's Spirit to heal this person's grief and help him find the peace he seeks.

We humans naturally tend to put a shortsighted emphasis on our earthly life—in the eternal scheme of things—and some consider death to be the ultimate negative scenario. From what I understand at this point, after my studies into near-death experiences, dying is not something to be feared like some dark alley—and neither is life. Grief for a deceased loved one (or any kind of loss for that matter) is a natural and normal reaction to the loss, but unresolved grief can turn into anger, bitterness, and frustration.

Sometimes there is a reasonable answer to a specific situation—like a body too broken to be resuscitated. But ultimately, I try to address the underlying question: "Doesn't God love me, too?" The answer is: "Absolutely yes, and God's love for you has *nothing* to do with 'misfortune' or 'entitlement.'"

Prayers that seem to go unanswered are a source of great disappointment for many. I've heard doubt-filled statements like, "I prayed to God for healing, but no healing came," or, "We have been praying for Jim to stop drinking, yet he hasn't changed."

AN ALIGNMENT OF WILLS

A few years ago our daughter Christina shared something with me. She said, "I've been praying for God to give me a horse this Christmas." As her father, I knew she was *not* getting a horse that Christmas. The circumstances just weren't right. A miracle for her would have been a terrible inconvenience for the rest of us. I tried my best to explain the big picture, so that the event of waking up Christmas morning and not finding a horse in the yard wouldn't affect her faith in God. But, I think this shows the limits of our human understanding of the big picture and our inability to mentally grasp the complexity of God's universe. We just can't see, from our limited perspective, the huge tapestry of interconnections between so many personal needs and the operations of nature that God manages.

The more I attempt to align my own free will with God's will, the more I find things working out for the good of everyone. But the question of *Why?* will always remain at the forefront of our simple minds as we desperately try to grasp how the God of the universe could love us so much that He would want to share His Spirit, His Light, with us. We're so trapped in the dim mind-set—our circumstances dictated by what we do or deserve—we often miss the light in the darkness. We glory in personal victory like a ticker tape parade in our own honor (not God's), and yet every setback is an excuse for us to build a higher, stronger wall around ourselves for protection.

CHAPTER EIGHT

THE IMPENETRABLE WALL

"But I say to you, love your enemies, bless those who
curse you, do good to those who hate you, and pray
for those who spitefully use you and persecute you."

—MATT. 5:44 NKJV

Stowe's Journey

The year 1971 was very special for me. I was ten years old when I made the acquaintance of a sweet little red-haired girl named Monica Cleary. We hit it off immediately, and for the first time I experienced what it was like to have a best friend. School became something I looked forward to; for it was there, on the playground and in between classes, that Monica and I could share our unique, off-the-wall humor—not to mention our deepest thoughts.

During class we drew pictures and notes, passing them back and forth to one another—much to the dismay of our teacher. We were frequently told to settle down and be quiet. Up to that point in my life I had never been a child to disobey the rules—I didn't like people to be disappointed in me; but for the first time in my life it didn't really matter. Nothing seemed more important to me than making Monica laugh.

Occasionally I was allowed to spend weekends with Monica. This, of course, was always a high time. Monica's family was very wealthy; I think her father was a lawyer. Their large home, surrounded by a black post fence and a few grazing horses, was located high atop a hill. The view was incredible.

But inside the great house I got the feeling life was not so perfect. Monica and her brother had intense fights that made me very uncomfortable to witness. There also seemed to be a sort of chasm between the parents and children. But none of this mattered much to me—I was there only to spend time with Monica.

In her bedroom we shared music, laughter, and our dreams. Our favorite dream was about our futures together. We had it all planned out: We would marry handsome men with beards. We even drew pictures of these bearded men, focusing on exactly what our own dream man would look like. (Interestingly, Peter looks just like the man I used to draw.) We planned to live in beautiful log cabins next to each other, and eat steak and drink champagne. Our lives as adults would be dreams come true.

One Friday after school I was waiting for my father to come and get me for the weekend. I was in a wonderful mood, until my foster father Joe came in and began talking with me. That day he was like a dark cloud of seriousness—talking about times in life that are difficult and how we sometimes have to be brave and get through them. I listened patiently with one ear, but was relieved when I finally saw my father pull into the driveway. *Enough of all this dreary talk! I'm ready to have some fun!*

I happily jumped into my Dad's car, only to find him in a bad mood as well. He nearly bit my head off in the first five minutes. So by the time we got to Dad's house, I was feeling pretty grumpy myself.

A few minutes after getting home, my father came into my room. He told me to sit down in a chair, and then he held out a handful of pills. Handing me a glass of water, he instructed me to take the pills. When I asked what they were for, he barked, "Just take them."

"But why?" I asked, not moving. "I'm not sick."

"Take them!" he ordered.

I swallowed hard, looked at the pills in his hand and then into his eyes. *Was he trying to kill me?* He gave me the pills and, after once more ordering me to take them, left the room. I looked down at the blue-and-white capsules in my hand. Scared and confused, I wondered if I should run away or maybe call Judy.

A few minutes later he came back into my room. When he saw I had still not taken the pills he became very angry, and we quickly became engaged in one of the most heated arguments we had ever had. But I stood my ground and he finally gave up. After seeing that he had lost the battle of the pills, he then ordered me into the living room. I was sitting on the sofa sobbing when he angrily stuck a newspaper clipping in my hand, and then went to pour himself a drink.

Through bleary eyes I slowly read the words:

Monica Cleary, 11, died Wednesday night at Memorial Hospital from a gunshot wound to the head. Her brother was blamed in the accidental shooting. Services will be held Saturday.

I sat there, speechless, my heart pounding wildly in my

chest, but I did not cry. I just stared at the newspaper clipping. My father soon reappeared and asked me if I wanted to go to the funeral. *Funeral? I'm afraid to go to funerals.* The Turners had taken me to the service of a baby. They had made me touch the small corpse—it was cold and hard and I didn't like it.

And now there was Monica, sweet Monica—no, I could not touch the dead body of my best friend. So, much to my father's disapproval, I decided not to go. I have regretted that decision many times since.

I was devastated by the loss of my best friend—I missed her terribly, but I didn't have a clue as to how to express my grief. Like everything else, I held it all inside. *Don't act too sad*, I would say to myself. *People die . . . that's life.*

It is only now, as I write this, that the tears are finally coming—in grief for my dear friend—more than thirty years later.

But life went on. Because the McDonalds built a new house farther out in the country, we started attending a new school, and life at a new school is never a picnic. I was teased and picked on and even earned the name "Witchy-poo" at one point. I don't know why children enjoyed picking on me. Perhaps it was because I was tall and skinny, and maybe I just looked like an easy target. Nevertheless, school days were hard, so I took solace in what became my new love—music.

My father played guitar, and so it came as no surprise to me or anyone else when I developed a love for that instrument. I got my first guitar at age eleven and almost immediately began composing songs. Self-taught, I have always joked that I spent nearly the entire decade of the seventies in my bedroom, playing my guitar—while in fact I was probably just tuning it. At one point I even had a twelve-string guitar.

At any rate, I wrote many songs, including one entitled "Hiding Behind My Guitar," which, looking back, was quite appropriately titled. My music and my guitar became my shield—a way to both express and cover up my deep and ever-present pain.

My father was either very supportive of my music or highly judgmental depending on his state of sobriety. One evening my latest song would be criticized, and on another I would be asked to perform it for visiting guests. As a consequence, I became terribly insecure and negative about my musical ability and, really, everything else I tried to do. Even these days, I occasionally still have to fight those negative voices—the evil ones that tell me I will fail; the ones that pressure me to compare myself and my work to everyone else's. I have worked hard to replace those messages with kinder words, and fortunately they're taking root.

One day in 1975, my father announced that it was time for me to come back home and live with him. This was about the worst news I could have ever heard. It never even entered my mind that I wouldn't be spending the rest of my childhood years with the McDonald family. The Mc-Donalds were brokenhearted as well, but what could we do? He was my father.

So at the age of fourteen and with the beginning of a new high school looming before me, I moved back in with my father. To say I hated him would be an understatement. As far as I could tell, he was bringing me home just to be a maid and cook for him. I found myself longing for the day when I would be an adult—anything had to be better than being a child with no control over my life.

But once I got over my initial adjustment, all was not so gloomy. On the bright side, my father and I had much in common—we loved music and spent hours talking about it, analyzing songs and singers and bands of the different eras. Movies and actors were also of great interest. Plus, we shared a goofy, cornball sense of humor that often kept us laughing late into the night. In many ways we were two peas in a superficial pod; never digging too deeply into either our spiritual or personal realms.

By the time I was in the tenth grade, my brother had been attending a school for the deaf for most of twelve years. But my father decided to bring him home and experiment with sending his deaf son to a hearing school. It was the first time this had ever been tried in our area, and it was very exciting having my brother at school with me. For the most part, people were very open to him—they liked him and wanted to understand and help him. For this reason I was sought out as his translator, and as a result I became much better known in school. I was Charles Dailey's sister—the only person who could understand him.

My self-esteem was boosted slightly by this new attention, but at home life was tense and stressful. My brother is a wonderful person, but back in those days he had a volatile temper, and he and my father fought intensely. I suspect the frustration of trying to live in a hearing world was too much for him. His relationship with Dad had never been an easy one. Whenever he saw a drink in Dad's hand (which was most of the time), Charles would point his finger and follow him around, yelling, "You always drink too much!" Down the hallway they would go with Charles screaming, "Drink, drink, drink! I do not like it!" And then Dad's door would slam, leaving Charles alone in the hall with his anger.

During these times I often locked myself in my room just to escape the commotion. Dad would even get in the car sometimes and go away for hours, leaving me to try and calm Charles. After a year and a half, it was decided that my brother was not learning as well as everyone had hoped. The experiment had failed, and Charles was sent to a state school for the deaf.

So I was left alone with Dad, both of us hiding behind the walls we'd built.

✳

Peter

Many of the worst scenarios in life become catalysts for positive change. Why would God allow Jesus, and other great men like Gandhi and Martin Luther King Jr., to die in such tragic ways? What good prospect could have been foreseen by Corrie Ten Boom in a Nazi concentration camp? Now consider the outcome their sufferings have had on the world.

Even the pain of divorce from my first wife caused me to seek healing, resulting in a long series of blessings. The apparent randomness of both blessings and hardships were a test of faith for me, and a reason to continue seeking God's Light for the journey.

Ultimately, our pains help us relate to other people's suffering and can allow God's healing power to connect us at an emotional level. Last year I showed some films to a group at a family camp. One woman stayed after the film and informed me that her eighteen-month-old nephew was accidentally killed in his stroller two weeks earlier when an elderly driver lost control of his car in a parking lot. The entire family was devastated by the loss of the child. The woman had a few soul-searching questions for me, and then she asked if we could pray for the parents. As we joined hands, all I could do was cry. At times, grieving is the only answer possible—and the only one necessary.

Being willing to stand in the gap with another person, wrestling with the good and the bad, is part of what it means to possess God's dangerous Spirit. Sometimes the good that results from the bad can help a world of people, as in the case of Martin Luther King Jr., and of course, Jesus Christ; while other times, it seems that only one person may be changed— as in the case of a brave woman named Marietta Jaeger.

COURAGE TO FORGIVE

I interviewed Marietta while producing a news story about the death penalty in Tennessee. Her life demonstrates a degree of forgiveness and healing that most people's lives could never approach.

Marietta had been in Nashville for a protest march called Journey of Hope, which presented several key speakers who were opposed to the death penalty. Among the notable panelists were Sister Helen Prejean (the Catholic nun who wrote *Dead Man Walking*) and Bill Walsh, whose daughter died in the Oklahoma City bombing. Most of the speakers built their cases upon the grounds that deliberately taking someone else's life is either ethically wrong or religiously immoral, whether that person is a murder victim or a death row convict.

Personally, I didn't feel strongly about the subject, and I could see both sides of reasoning on the issue. Ms. Jaeger's story, however, affected me emotionally because God had touched her in a way that defies all logical reasoning.

More than twenty-five years ago, Marietta Jaeger's seven-year-old daughter Susie had been kidnapped while on a family camping trip in Wyoming. As the family slept, a drifter had crept into camp and quietly cut a hole in the side of the canvas tent. Without waking a soul, the young man plucked the little girl from her sleep and vanished into the night.

The next morning, police and news crews scoured the area. Susie's young mother held back tears while telling news reporters of her desperation. Posters of the missing girl were plastered throughout the surrounding areas.

Finally, a week after the abduction, the kidnapper contacted the Jaeger family through the local sheriff's office. The caller identified Susie by an unpublished birth defect and said he wanted to exchange the little girl for ransom. Tragically, the man never placed a second call, so the Jaeger family stayed in the campground, unable to return home. They had nothing to do but wait.

"During that time," Marietta recalled in our interview many years later, "while the investigation and search and questioning of suspects ensued, I really got in touch with my rage and hatred for this person—whoever he was—and my desire to have him executed, because I knew the penalty for kidnapping in that state was the death penalty. I was seething with hate, ravaged with a desire for revenge. 'Even if Susie were brought back to us alive and well,' I would tell my husband, 'I could kill that man,' and I meant it with every fiber of my being."

As I dug deeper into Marietta's old news clippings and film footage to gather material for my report, I could feel my own blood boiling and tears welling up. It was not hard to adopt the family's rage and desperation, as I considered my own two little girls, and I felt the darkness enshrouding my own imaginary lapse into that family's nightmare.

I sat speechless as I played and replayed the scratchy old news clip of the drained young mother reciting, "We haven't given up hope yet. We can do nothing else. We have simply put her in God's hands and prayed that He will keep her safe and return her to us. And if Susie is suffering, we pray that He takes her so that she will be spared any more . . ." This began a mother's unimaginable search to recover the child that had been ripped from her.

That prayer, Marietta later explained to me, was just the beginning of a long journey and a series of inward battles. "As a Catholic Christian, I recognized that I was called to *forgive* this person. . . ." yet she told herself that to forgive the kidnapper would mean betraying her daughter. But Marietta also realized that no amount of anger was going to bring her daughter home, and she deeply sensed that forgiveness may be the only way she could personally survive her own self-consuming grief. So, she continued to pray that God would forgive the man, and that He would give her strength to release her rage as well: "Lord, You have to forgive this man for me . . . because I can't do it on my own."

The final test came without warning, in the same manner the kidnapper had struck the previous year. "One year to the minute in which he had taken Susie out of our tent—in the middle of the night—the man called me at my home in Michigan. And it was quickly clear that he was really calling to taunt me. He wanted to tell me, 'Here I am, now what do you want to do about it? Because you're never going to find out who I am.' "

There was a long pause, and when Marietta finally opened her mouth to answer the man who had caused her family such terrible suffering, the voice that came out may have sounded like hers . . . but it was God speaking.

Marietta explained, "In spite of the fact that the kidnapper was being very smug and nasty, I realized that all the things I had been working for in that intervening year—moving my heart toward forgiveness—was coming to fruition in me, and he was undone by that."

Her response to the man shocked him—and herself as well. She didn't get angry with him, but instead turned the conversation around to talk about how much pain he, himself, must have suffered in his life, to make him commit such a crime. She engaged the kidnapper with compassion, and he became very emotional, crying and talking with her as one would a trusted friend.

Eventually, through subsequent phone calls, the kidnapper shared enough information to be tracked down and apprehended by the FBI. He was tried and convicted of murder, at which point Marietta asked that he receive maximum life imprisonment with no chance of parole rather than face the death penalty. After a short time in prison, David—who was diagnosed as schizophrenic—took his own life.

Ms. Jaeger's remarkable turnaround became the subject of a book, *Out of the Darkness*, in which she describes the process of forgiving the man who had, in fact, murdered Susie and several other children. "All the time we were searching for her, she was already safely home in the arms of God."

Marietta still refers to her daughter's killer simply as "David," in order to spare his own family further grief. Marietta now travels the world, attending lectures and rallies and protesting against the death penalty. She is outspoken about her story of healing from the self-destructive hatred that tends to haunt the families of murder victims.

"My own healing would have been rendered impossible if Susie's offender had been executed on account of my desire for vengeance. . . . I'd already had fifteen months to process my feelings about this, and I had come to the realization that to kill somebody in Susie's name would be to violate and profane the goodness, sweetness, and beauty of her life. And I realized I would be violating her by memorializing her death with another death, another killing, which would make another victim and another grieving family."[1]

I'm sure some people would be mystified by Marietta's dramatic change of heart. It would be easy to simply write off her transformation as a symptom of weakness, succumbing to the grief of her great loss. However, I looked into her eyes and saw the amazing character of one whose soul didn't disintegrate from her terrible tragedy, but instead was healed and grew stronger by accepting God's guidance to forgive. Her warm smile radiates love and compassion from a place of deep security.

Like so many people who suffer the results of tragedy, Marietta could have built a wall of grief and anger around herself. Instead she stood beside David and wrestled his demons with him. That kind of love is all that God asks of us.

CHAPTER NINE

WRESTLING WITH GOD

*My people have been lost sheep: their shepherds
have caused them to go astray; they have turned
them away on the mountains; they have gone from
mountain to hill; they have forgotten their
resting-place.*

—JER. 50:6 ASV

Stowe's Journey

In 1976, an amazing and wonderful thing happened to
me, and as a result my life was forever changed. An on-
fire Christian neighbor invited me to a hot, crowded re-
vival hall on the outskirts of town. It was there, high up in
the bleachers of an old auditorium, that I discovered the exciting and powerful love of Jesus for the first time. This
enormous love was far more than I could fathom (in fact, it
still is), but that night I opened my arms wide and did my
best to receive it.

I asked God to come into my heart, and as I did I began
releasing to Him some of the pain I had carried for much of
my young life. I couldn't hold back the tears as I received
the forgiveness I so deeply needed. There were also tears of
joy that flowed from deep within me as I suddenly realized
there was more to life than just me, my family, and this old

earth. I became aware, too, that in my eyes I had always seen myself as unclean and therefore totally unworthy of anything good. But now, not only was something good happening to me, but something totally incredible—right there in my chair, among all those people. God's love was igniting a fire within my heart.

It was an unforgettable moment.

The euphoria I experienced from my Christ encounter lasted for weeks, and I immediately bought a Bible and began studying God's Word. It was a King James Version, and even though it wasn't an easy read, I plodded on. I also began praying on a regular basis, even though this presented a different struggle—I found it difficult to pray for myself. It was easier praying mostly for other people because I still did not feel deserving enough to pray for my own wants and needs. I was learning a great deal about the power of God but, even so, I was still being tested from many directions.

There was alcohol and pornography in our home, and a world around me whose morals were all but forgotten. I was trying to be what I thought was a good Christian, but it wasn't easy.

I spent some weekends with the McDonalds here and there, and was saddened when I found out that Judy and Joe were getting a divorce. But nothing could have prepared me for the news I received one day concerning my foster brother, Joey.

Judy called me, her voice unusually shaky. "Honey," she began softly but bravely. "I've got some bad news. Joey has testicular cancer and . . . and it's very serious." He was seventeen—the same age as me.

Judy and Joey set forth on a brave battle against a disease

that is ruthless. They traveled to various hospitals around the state as Joey endured operations and numerous treatments. He continued with school and, despite his cancer and treatment, acted in school plays, graduated with honors, and wrote beautiful poetry that showed perception beyond his years. I was happy to be able to visit him from time to time.

During my last year of high school, Dad was laid off from his job of twenty-six years. Money was tight, and I was told if I wanted to attend college I would have to go to a state school and work to pay for it. Other than music, I had no idea what I wanted to do, and the idea of working just to go to school did not appeal to me.

I think I was hungry just to get out into the world and make some mistakes by my own hand for a while. So I took a third-shift job waiting tables, moved back in with Judy, and was off and running.

The days of trying to be a good Christian faded to a memory as I ventured out into the night world. I had tried churchgoing regularly with my friends, but in the end I had felt overwhelmed by it all. There was such turmoil within my soul, and somehow the heavy-handed teachings of the church I had attended only served to make me feel worse. I simply could not live up to the high standards that were being set for me. I was a wounded sinner, unable to accept love from anyone—not even God.

It was around this time that Judy asked me to help take care of Joey—things were getting rough for him. He had developed leukemia in early 1980, and when we brought him home from the hospital, we set up a hospital bed in Judy's room. Judy's sister Rose also came to help.

I'll never forget that cold spring morning in March when Joey finally gave up his two-year-long battle with cancer. I remember the paramedics carrying his body outside while a soft, gentle snow began to fall. I broke down for the first time, realizing that one of the sweetest and most talented people I had ever met was gone.

Life without him would never be the same.

Watching Judy, I saw firsthand how devastating the loss of a child could be to a mother. She lost so much of her spark after that.

Meanwhile, I became even more convinced that those you love the most are often the ones that die young. So somewhere, deep inside myself, I resolved once again not to get too close to anyone. I knew that would make for a lonely life, but that was my battle to fight.

✦

When God is about to do something great, He starts with a difficulty. When He is about to do something truly magnificent, He starts with an impossibility.

—ARMIN GESSWEIN

Peter

Many of the stories I studied for the show *Miracles, Angels & Afterlife* have also emphasized the power of the Holy Spirit as it relates to physical and emotional healing. Just who or what is this mysterious presence called the Holy Spirit, and where does it fit into the picture of God's power to mend lives? I truly believe that if we seek an honest answer to the question

"Who or what is the Holy Spirit?" we will find a major key to unlocking the great mystery of miraculous healing and the very gateway to God's loving power.

But personally, there were people in my life that held the idea of the Holy Spirit hostage. They dangled it in front of me like a carrot on a string and led me far from the truth of His true Light.

THE DARK ROAD TO TRUTH

As a young Christian, I was hungry for anything that God and Jesus could teach me about the power of love. When I read in the Bible about the gifts of the spirit (1 Corinthians 13) and how *love* was the greatest of all the gifts, I knew I was zeroing in on the essence of spiritual purity, so I gravitated toward a style of worship that emphasized the gifts of the *Holy Spirit* like speaking in tongues, prophecy, interpretation, healing, and other so-called manifestations. In those days this form of worship was referred to as the charismatic renewal.

One meeting I attended regularly on Wednesday nights was with one of those so-called charismatic renewal groups, and it was truly a wonderful gathering. When I first attended, it met at the Homewood Recreation Center in suburban Maryland with around twenty teenagers and adult leaders. Two leaders in particular were especially gifted teachers who could make scriptures come to life and in whom the Spirit of God shone brightly. Within a couple years this group had become so immensely popular that it moved to the large Christ Church in Washington, D.C., where two thousand people would gather to enjoy the beautifully angelic harmonies of singing "in the

Spirit," sharing in this charismatic style of worship that seemed so refreshing in the early seventies.

Eventually I moved to Annapolis with my family and looked for a new church there. I hoped to find a group emphasizing the gifts of the Holy Spirit to feed my spiritual hunger like the other group in Washington, D.C., had done. What I found was a more rural charismatic church, but it contained much the same outward style of worship. What I didn't understand until much later was that it belonged to a larger, quasi-franchised organization known as the Shepherding Movement. Our local pastor was a zealous officer from the U.S. Naval Academy, and he led the group like a ship's captain. Followers would be shepherded in their political choices, their career paths, and their selection of spouses. I felt protected by the *discipleship* system, in which an older member would take a youth under his or her wing.

My own mother attended this church for a while. However, one Sunday morning she was chastised publicly for speaking up and questioning the leadership's authority to instruct the followers on how to vote in an upcoming election. She was told that a woman was expected to remain submissive to the elders, even though she was by far their elder in years. Suffice it to say, Mom quickly changed churches.

I grew wary of the leadership of the church, but I still attended. The last straw for me came when the local "shepherding" pastor called a meeting with my girlfriend and me. He explained how God had told him we should marry, and how it was better to wed than burn in lust. What he *didn't* hear from God was how this girl and I were extremely unsuited for one another, and a marriage between us would be absolutely disastrous. Fortunately, my father, who had lost patience with the shepherding church, explained to me that, based on his own experience with a previous marriage, it would be crazy to marry someone I was already having conflicts with. (Thank you, Dad!)

So I made a clean break from the herd and vowed never to be shepherded again. And after this bitter experience—in a typically youthful act of rebellion—I fell away from anything with the word Christian attached . . . for nearly ten years. It was during that decade of whiplash that I sank into a mire of drugs, drinking, and general debauchery.

Many years later I discovered, to no great surprise, that the local shepherding pastor had served time in jail (for misuse of funds, I think), and that the whole infrastructure of the Shepherding Movement had imploded amidst great scandal. I also learned, incidentally, that the local shepherding pastor had paid a visit to my previous church in D.C., which I had loved so much, and it was disbanded as a result—something about creating too much competition with the local shepherding branches.

God only knows how many other *sheep* were led astray by this Christian cult.

There now . . . I've said it. I was part of a religious cult. This was probably one of the greatest disappointments in my life, and it took a big bite out of my faith and spiritual growth for a very long time. I suppose that anybody who has turned over his or her personal will and freedom of conscience to any kind of cult and then woken up to the mistake must develop some distrust of any and all organized religion.

In my case, I had a difficult time looking squarely at reports of people who claimed to be "anointed" by the Holy Spirit, or who claimed to get their messages directly from God. So-called faith healers and other evangelical showmen of the world operate in a limelight that I still cannot fairly explore without an overwhelming burden of my own baggage of prejudice.

One of my favorite Old Testament prophecies speaks of a day when people would no longer require strict religious supervision, because the Spirit of the Lord will be found in everyone's hearts. Ironically, it is the verse where the strictly regimented shepherding church I just described got its name, New Covenant:

> *"The time is coming" declares the LORD, "when I*
> *will make a new covenant with the house of Israel*
> *and with the house of Judah. . . . I will put my law*
> *in their minds and write it on their hearts. I will be*
> *their God, and they will be my people. No longer*
> *will a man teach his neighbor, or a man his*
> *brother, saying. 'Know the LORD,' because they will*
> *all know me, from the least of them to the greatest,"*
> *declares the LORD. "For I will forgive them their*
> *wickedness and will remember their sins no more."*
>
> —JER. 31:31, 33–34 NIV

I knew in my heart that hearing the Spirit is a potent and profound reality that is available to everyone. And I also knew if I was going to allow that spiritual power to flow unobstructed in my life, I had to get over my own personal feelings of distrust. But, I needed to approach it from a different angle. I avoided books, TV shows, and other media that relied on the typical jargon and catchphrases referred to as the language of "Christianese" (Christian-ease). I attempted to find a fresh look at spirituality. I wanted to see from a perspective that wasn't bogged down by easy religious definitions.

Although there were times when I appeared to have fought and given up on God (much like Stowe during her wrestling matches with God), I now see that He never gave up on either of us. He charted an unusual course for our individual and united lives.

As a result of the paths He took us on, our deepest convictions were given new clarity. We have gained a more restful understanding of the nature of God's Light. We've continued to wrestle with the concepts of judgment and forgiveness. And we rest more deeply now in the reality of the Holy Spirit's presence. We believe these things are vital to us all in this dangerous and unholy world.

CHAPTER TEN

A PLACE TO GROW

But he said to me, "My grace is sufficient for you,
for my power is made perfect in weakness."
Therefore I will boast all the more gladly about my
weaknesses, so that Christ's power may rest on me.

—2 COR. 12:9 NIV

Stowe's Journey

After Joey's death, the next few years of my life were spent running aimlessly—trying to find myself. But the more I looked, the less I liked what I saw. I had a string of broken relationships; in fact, my motto was: Always be the first to leave. I wasn't leaving on a jet plane, but I sure didn't know when I'd be back again.

It was too depressing for me to stay in Asheville, so I moved to Charlotte, North Carolina, where my days were spent waiting tables, and my nights were wasted in clubs and bars—always looking but never finding. *Who was I? Why was I?*

In bed, late at night, I would toss and turn as scenes from my childhood played over and over in my head. I did not speak of these things—not to anyone, not even to God. I was definitely a lost soul.

It was around this time that Judy called me. She told me she had gone to dinner with my father and his girlfriend the previous night, and she was furious with him. He had been drinking heavily during dinner and talking about what a wonderful son he had—how well Charles was doing in school and how proud he was of him. He then switched subjects and, with bitterness in his voice, began talking about what a disappointment I was to him. In his eyes, apparently, I would never be more than an uneducated waitress. I was wasting my life and would never amount to anything.

Judy, the only person who knew about my experience at the Turners, couldn't hold back any longer. "Well, Dick, did you know that your daughter was sexually molested when she was only six years old by that Turner man?"

Dad leaned back in his chair a little. "Well," he said slowly, "those things happen. . . ."

Stunned by his response, Judy left the table in tears and ran to the bathroom. My father's girlfriend followed her.

Hearing this story hurt me deeply, and it felt like the final straw with my father. I had stood up for him my whole life, doing my best to defend him when others put him down. I had rarely said anything against him.

But those days were over now. If he didn't care about me any more than that, I saw no reason why I should care about him.

Over the next few years I made virtually no effort to stay in touch with my father. I did see him from time to time at family reunions, and he called me occasionally; but we spoke only on a superficial level as my heart was closed to him.

In my early twenties something strange began happening to me. I was beginning to have moments when I felt as if something in my brain was disconnecting. I would be unable to speak, and it was hard to keep my eyes open. Afterward I would feel tired and, given the opportunity, I would sleep for hours. I told several doctors about my symptoms, but no one was able to diagnose it. Seven years passed before I learned I had epilepsy. My father, in fact, was the one who figured it out.

In the meantime, I felt very embarrassed by these little spells. What little confidence I had was eroding—I hated for anyone to see me like this. *What was wrong with me? Why was I so strange?* Depression was a regular part of my life, and I occasionally toyed with the idea of suicide, but fortunately I just didn't have the courage to pull it off.

At the age of twenty-two, though, I had yet another life-changing experience—one that I must give credit to God for arranging. A friend and I were going out to celebrate our mutual birthdays in her Volkswagen Beetle when we were hit head-on by a drunk driver in a van. My friend was severely hurt—arm and facial injuries kept her out of work for nearly a year, while I suffered only minor injuries—a broken nose and foot. But it was during my time of recovery that some deeper healing began.

As I recuperated on the sofa, I realized if I had died that night, my life would have been for nothing. I had not utilized any of my talents, and even though I hardly spoke to my father at that time, deep down inside I did care what he thought about me. Even though my dad was an alcoholic, he still had high standards for character, accomplishment, and conduct. I knew I had fallen way below his expectations—and now I realized I had fallen below my own.

In Search of My Voice

So I began focusing on my music, writing, and singing. I was introduced to some people who were putting together a country band, and soon we were playing in clubs—I was actually making money with my music! One band led to another, and somewhere along the way I met a woman who really believed in me. Her name was Gail Strawn.

Gail and I became great friends, and together we began planning for my future as a country singer. With her encouragement, I worked hard at improving both my songwriting skills and strengthening my vocal abilities.

It was around this time that I decided to drop my first name—Anne—and begin using only my middle and last name—Stowe Dailey. With this change, I felt as if I had loosed my shackles. I was starting over and beginning a new path that would leave behind the little girl named Anne—the child who had been a victim of circumstances beyond her control. I see now that this was one of my first steps toward building a new identity, and though it was a good one, I would later learn that it takes more than a name change to overcome the past.

I may have been trying to forget my past, but my friend Gail was set on reconnecting me with it. In fact, she was the main reason my father and I were able to rekindle our relationship. I'll never forget the night they met in a club where I was playing—it was an instantaneous friendship.

She loved my father and he loved her. Soon after their meeting, she became intent on getting us back together. It's kind of amazing how it all worked out: They began plotting my rise to stardom together, and soon he was driving down to Charlotte to spend the weekend and come to my shows. Through Gail's efforts, Dad and I got to know and trust one another again.

Eventually, Gail and I formed a four-piece road band, and I toured the western and northern United States and Canada. It was hard work and great fun. What an experience! But a year on the road was enough for me to know that it was only leading to a dead end; so my band and I came off the road in 1986. After a few months off, Gail and I set our sights on Nashville, Tennessee.

By 1987, I had rented an apartment on the fourth floor of the Spence Manor on Sixteenth Avenue. Imagine—a little ol' mountain girl taking up residence on Music Row. It was a pretty exciting time for me; my voice and songwriting abilities had come a long way over the last few years. I was fortunate enough to meet some pretty influential people right off the bat, too, so I was able to write with some of the best songwriters Nashville had to offer.

I also did a few recordings of my material and presented myself before a few of the big producers. But after almost two years—and no lucrative offers on the table—I decided to focus my full attention on songwriting. Part of the reason for this decision had to do with a then unknown singer-songwriter named Garth Brooks.

The year was 1989; Garth and I and another mutual friend, Kim Williams, occasionally hung out together. Kim suggested that Garth and I write together—and so we did. One night after we had been hammering out a song for a few hours, Garth wandered over to the large picture win-dow overlooking Sixteenth Avenue. Just a few weeks away from beginning his first tour of the States to promote his new album, he was in a very pensive mood. He admitted he was nervous about his future, but what really struck me was his resolve to make it . . . and make it *big*. He said he wanted to be more successful than George Jones. Well, now, I have to say that, at the time, it seemed like a bit of a mission impossible. I mean, he was a really good singer with some great songs . . . but, *bigger than George Jones?* This was quite some talk, some big belief in himself—something I knew I lacked.

Because of that conversation, I came to the realization over the next few weeks that perhaps being a famous singer at the top of the pyramid wasn't something I was cut out for. Besides, I had met quite a few famous people during my stay in Nashville, and their lives weren't nearly as glamorous as they looked on the outside. There's a lot of pressure on the top person to succeed—a little too much for my fragile personality.

A week or so later, Garth invited me to an incredible show he was doing for his record label where I actually saw for the first time the spark that was soon to ignite him into one of the world's most entertaining singers—one who would indeed surpass George Jones and nearly any-one else in the world. During the middle of the show, he stopped to thank a few key people at his record label, and he also mentioned two up-and-coming singers. One of them was the very talented Trisha Yearwood (who recently became his second wife), and the other was me. I was shocked, to say the least; and very honored. But even this vote of confidence from one so talented as Garth Brooks was not enough to change my negative attitude about my-self.

And so, much to the dismay of many people, I made my mind up—I would pursue a career in songwriting. To me, it felt like the most natural thing in the world, and I wasn't asking for much—just a chance to be creative with my songs and hopefully earn a living singing and playing *outside* of the limelight. It seemed to me all I needed in order to grow was a small pot and a sweet spot in the sun—and a little love.

✦

> *Hope is much more than a mood. It involves a*
> *commitment to action . . . What we hope for should*
> *be what we are prepared to work for and so bring*
> *about, as far as that power lies in us.*
> —JOHN POLKINGHORNE

Peter

Life seems to be lived in cycles—ups and downs. Hopes, dreams, disappointments—and healing. Stowe and I both experienced our share of all those things before we met, and once we found each other, we continued to go through all the familiar cycles of life. Only now, we were going through them together.

SHADES OF DESPAIR AND HOPE

In an earlier chapter, I shared my anguish about the difficulties we faced with my television career and the overall frustration of living in today's world. It's hard to believe, at the time of this writing, that it's been more than five years since the tragic occurrence of September 11—a time when most of the world stopped to take inventory.

Stowe and I moved our family out of our small converted barn and into our newly completed house on Christmas Eve of 2001. Waking up in our dream home on Christmas morning was the most wonderful gift imaginable! Seeing the girls coming down the stairs in their pajamas for the first time is a picture we'll never forget—even though the Christmas tree was standing on a still bare plywood floor. Never mind all the work we had left to do . . . at least we were warm and cozy! But the gladness of the holiday, and the incredible journey we had been on that year, was mixed with a sense of worry. The construction budget, which had kept us afloat while Stowe and I completed the tasks of building our house, was now virtually gone. The experience of doing the contracting, carpentry, painting, and everything else had given us lots of part-time jobs, but it had also prevented me from seriously pursuing any new television work. Now that our home was built, we had a sizable mortgage but no income on the horizon.

I did my best to continue pitching ideas for television shows . . . documentaries, TV series, specials . . . but the doors kept shutting. It seemed like a blanket of fear had covered the television industry, and nobody was willing to spend money on new programs.

In March 2002 we got an exciting call from some friends near Knoxville. They told us of a new entertainment and media complex they were involved in developing, and they asked if I would be interested in helping build and run the TV studio. After several very encouraging trips and meetings, backing for the entire project fell apart and we were back to searching.

I laid awake nights. My imagination was in high gear, re-playing the scenarios of our recent past, our precarious pres-ent, and our unfocused future. It looked like our worst fears might be coming true. After struggling for years—and then reaching our goals of producing uplifting TV shows, building the home of our dreams, and establishing our children's home-school pattern—it now seemed likely that we could lose it all.

The worst part was that I felt I'd somehow let down my family—and God. "Lord . . . I've done everything I can hu-manly think of doing!" I prayed urgently. "Please, if there is something that I have overlooked—if I've left a stone un-turned—show me."

Dark thoughts flashed through my soul: *Perhaps the best thing would be for me to have a heart attack, or a fatal wreck . . . at least the life insurance would provide for my family.* Although I knew I would never take my own life, it slapped me in the face to consider I might be more valuable dead than alive. Deep down in my heart, I knew my daughters needed both their father and mother more than they needed a nice house or money.

Then, one Tuesday, I got a message that sounded like a voice from heaven. Two of my coproducers and close friends, Fred Rowles and Gene Smith, met with me as we had every week, just to help keep each other on track after our series *Miracles, Angels & Afterlife* had been canceled the year before. Together we had valiantly sought new avenues for our shows and pitched future projects—with no results.

On this particular Tuesday, after sharing another home-made lunch that we took turns providing, Fred announced, "Well, I think I heard a message from God last night." Of course, he had our attention. "In my time of prayer, a clear thought came to me," Fred continued. "I had the strong feeling that the work we did is successfully finished. We don't need to keep pursuing the same path anymore, because that chapter is completed. I think God wants us to know that He is proud of what we did and should consider it a 'job well done!' "

I don't know whether an angel whispered this to Fred, but I do know one thing: It was just what I needed to hear. I had been on the same track for more than ten years, investigating supernatural experiences of people touched by heavenly encounters. In fact, I was so blessed by studying and sharing these stories, I never considered doing anything else. And until Fred shook me awake, suggesting it might really be the end for that leg of the journey, I hadn't allowed God to lead me anywhere else.

Suddenly I understood that I didn't need to feel like I was traveling alone. God would continue to guide me. Finally, I understood that we were indeed at the right place at the right time. I stopped feeling like a failure and a has-been, and I gratefully acknowledged the time I was being given to recharge my batteries.

But even with the new peace of mind from letting go of past missions, I still had bills to pay. By now we had spent every dime in our bank account, and we were charging groceries on credit cards.

We considered building houses professionally. The experience of constructing our country farmhouse gave us courage to explore the feasibility of building "spec" homes. But the risk of having a finished house sit on the market was high at that time, and I found banks unwilling to extend our already stretched credit for such a speculative project.

I faced the uncomfortable prospect of getting a home equity loan, or second mortgage, just to pay our mounting debts. Although we have faced similar pinches in the past, the mere thought gave me sweaty palms. *Should we sell the house and cut our losses?* Stowe and I talked and prayed about it, but we agreed it was too early to give up the ship.

Nervously, I called the number on some junk mail I had received that advertised a "low interest, home-equity line of credit." I spoke to a cheerful and personable woman, who turned out to have once gone to a church we previously attended. Although we agreed her company's interest rates were too high for my needs, she referred me to another broker she knew from her current church. I then called her friend and explained my situation. Not only did this second broker assure me that she indeed could arrange a loan, but also said in passing, "And whenever you want to consider *real estate investing,* I can introduce you to a great realtor. But for now . . ."

"Wait a minute . . ." I interrupted. "Tell me more about this real estate investing."

I got a name and number, and I was soon speaking with an experienced investment realtor. She described a business I had never considered—buying old houses, renovating them, and then either selling or renting them. I absorbed every word, and I quickly understood the various strategies. That night, when I told Stowe about what I'd learned, it caught her imagination, too, in view of our mutual fascination with old houses. We decided to look into it further.

God led us, through a series of introductions, to some talented investors who showed us a whole new business; different from anything we had conceived of before. After the great experience of building our new vintage farmhouse together, Stowe and I immediately took to the venture of rehabbing genuinely old houses. We began buying old properties, fixing them up, and helping to renovate previously run-down neighborhoods. Although it isn't a get-rich-quick business, it gradually helped us get on our feet. And we are constantly seeing ways our efforts have helped other people, too.

Eventually, new projects did come. I coproduced a wonderful documentary called "Prophecies of the Passion" for TBN; and another called "A Journey Home," which won Best Documentary Award at the San Antonio Independent Christian Film Festival. Stowe and I also put our writing skills to work in cowriting *The Hallelujah Diet,* for which I also produced a series of videos. Through all these new experiences, the Lord has turned the disappointment of the past into excitement for future opportunities.

My Maker knows me, and He always knows best where to lead my heart. I just had to learn to wait for His call.

Stowe

As far as Peter's previous feeling of disconnection from what he had believed to be God's desire for his life—fortunately, my husband has a rock-solid faith built upon his own unforgettable Christ-encounter as a teenager. His eyes still sparkle whenever he shares his story about the day he invited Jesus into his heart. His spirit was filled with an incredible love and his life was forever changed. Only weeks after meeting Jesus, he began a film career in which he would explore further the wonderful gift he had received.

Over the years Peter's film work has led him to meet and interview dozens of people who have inspired not only him but many others with their accounts of miraculous physical, spiritual, and emotional healing. These stories have encouraged us time and time again, letting us know that the power of God's healing Light is at work in the world every moment of every day, reaching out to us all through dreams, stories, compassion, empathetic sensitivity, and everyday insights. Even during dark times, when we feel the light at the end of the tunnel is only the headlight of an oncoming train, we can rest in the assurance that the dim light we see at the time is the Spirit of God within us—burning bright and guiding us home.

CHAPTER ELEVEN

THE PATH TO PERFECT UNION

*The LORD will work out his plans for my life—for
your faithful love, O LORD, endures forever. Don't
abandon me, for you made me.*

—PSALMS 138:8 NLT

Stowe's Journey

By the time 1989 rolled around, I was firmly rooted in Music Row. My daily routine involved sorting baseball cards for extra money, occasionally going out with friends, and, of course, songwriting. I was regularly in the company of some impressive, up-and-coming songwriters. For the most part I was enjoying my life in Nashville.

But the nights were sometimes lonely. At almost twenty-eight years of age I had yet to meet the man of my dreams, and I was beginning to have the feeling that perhaps I was destined to remain a single woman.

I was thinking along these lines one day when I made a significant decision—it was time to reestablish my relationship with God. I felt compelled to do this and I actually got down on my knees and, asking for forgiveness, gave my life back to God. I told God I would leave it up to Him to decide whom I should marry—and even *if* I should marry. Afterward I felt a tremendous peace, and I decided I would definitely like to pray more often.

It was only two weeks later that I got a call from a girl-friend, Charlu, asking me if I'd like to go to the movies with her and another friend of ours, Gene Smith. I said, "Sure."

"Oh, by the way," she said, "there's a cute guy named Peter coming with us. . . . You might like him." I could just hear the smile in her voice.

"Uh, no, thanks," I said quickly. "I'm not looking for anyone."

Why is it that you find the most incredible treasures when you're not looking for them? I've yet to figure that one out, but just a few hours later I was crawling into the backseat of Gene's Isuzu Trooper and coming face-to-face with my future husband—a handsome man with a beard (*wink, wink, Monica!*)

That night we went to see a comedy called *The Dream Team.* Boy, did we have fun! Peter and I talked and joked so much through the movie we had to rent it again the next year just to see what we missed. But the moniker *Dream Team* was not lost on us—we've called ourselves that since almost the day we met.

Life suddenly became very exciting. Over the next few months our relationship blossomed, and so did my relationship with God. I began handing over more and more of the big decisions in my life to Him (I had yet to discover that He could also handle the small stuff). Of course, I prayed about Peter. *Is this the right man for me, Lord? If he is, let me know it in my heart.* And that peaceful feeling came to me again.

A year and a half after we met, Peter Shockey and I were married in Hendersonville, North Carolina. Dad took great joy in planning the whole wedding and, of course, it was quite the party. We've been married now for almost seventeen years and I am ever grateful for the husband God chose for me. Over the years, his patience and wisdom and love for the Lord have helped light my path and, as a result, my life on earth and my walk with God have only gotten stronger.

But it has not been without trial. The wounds of my past have often bled over into our marriage, and there have been many times of depression for me.

In the early years of our marriage, Peter often commented that I was responding to him much in the same way I had always responded to my father—from the position of a victim. I frequently shot down his ideas for seemingly no reason. I had no answers or ideas of my own to give him—only teary eyes. Looking back now, I can see what a fearful person I was—afraid of losing ground, afraid of being misunderstood, and most of all, afraid of being forgotten. I know it was very frustrating for Peter to have to deal with the demons of my past, and I am so grateful to him for standing by me and doing battle with me. My confidence in my own abilities was weak, and I questioned every endeavor I undertook, often talking myself out of succeeding at things before I had even begun! Even my success as a songwriter was not enough to override the taunting voices that tricked me into comparing myself to every other songwriter on earth. And my dreams were no safe haven, either.

By now Garth's incredible megastardom began dogging me in recurring nightmares. The scenario was almost always the same; Garth, myself, and some friends would be hanging out together having fun, usually in a hallway, when they would all be called into another room, where there was an important Music Row party going on. I was never invited. My self-esteem plummeted further. At that time I just couldn't seem to win against the negative inner voices—they were too strong.

Fortunately, though, I was not completely paralyzed. I did have enough gumption to have pursued many of my dreams, including a moderately successful music career and eventually having children.

One of the highlights of my life has definitely been the gift of our two beautiful daughters, but I would have never known such a gift had it not been for the grace of God and a miraculous intervention that was about to take place.

A Maternal Gift

For as long as I could remember I had been against the idea of having children. They simply weren't on my to-do list. From time to time I had tried to imagine it, but I always concluded that I wasn't "mother material." Just thinking about it made me extremely uneasy. In fact, I recall something that happened in the early days of mine and Peter's relationship.

Gail, my music manager, had just met him and she wanted to know what Peter saw when he looked at me (of course, she was hoping he would say a big country music star). He gazed up at me with dreamy eyes and said, "I think Stowe would be a wonderful mother." Well, I just about fell off the sofa trying to get as far away from him as possible. *What was he thinking?* (Very positive thoughts, I would later discover).

For the first few years of our marriage, conversations about children were rare—we were both busy with our work. But over time I became less enamored with the *business* of songwriting. Somehow it just didn't feel right to me anymore. I began looking for other ways to satisfy my musical itch. And I also started praying for wisdom about what to do with my life.

One morning I was talking with some friends who were visiting when something strange happened to me. We were in my office chatting, while across the house I could hear the sounds of their little girl making a mess in our kitchen. This was particularly annoying to me (in fact, it reminded me of one of the very reasons why I didn't want to have children). I stared deep into their eyes, trying hard to focus on our conversation.

All of a sudden, from somewhere to my left, I heard a female voice; it was outside of my head and in first person. "*I want to have a baby,*" it said. I was shocked, but I didn't give it a second thought before I answered.

"*No, I don't!*" I shot back silently. From across the house I could still hear the racket their little girl was making in the kitchen.

"*I want to have a baby,*" the voice persisted.

"*No, I don't!*" I said emphatically.

Our friends were totally unaware of this silent conversation, and I hadn't a clue as to what they were talking about, either. All I knew was that for the first (and only) time in my life, I had heard a voice and it had planted the seeds of motherhood deep into my psyche.

For the rest of the morning I walked around in a daze. After our friends left, I surveyed the damage done by their little girl—it would take me a while to clean it all up. *That,*

I confirmed to myself, *is why I don't want to have children. So there!*

Later that morning I made my usual rounds to drop off tapes of my songs. First I went by Reba McEntire's publishing company. Upon my arrival I was greeted by the receptionist, who was soon expecting her first baby. She was just full of excitement at the prospect of being a mother—she could hardly wait to see her new baby. Another woman, a new mother, walked up and chimed in about the joys of motherhood. She said she was looking forward to having another one. Songwriters passing by the desk also began relating stories of how satisfying it was to be a parent. I'm sure I was standing there with my mouth open. I couldn't help but wonder, *Was I missing something?* I mean, grown men were nearly crying while talking about their children. *Could it really be that wonderful?*

As I drove away, I began to open my mind to the possibility of motherhood. When I got to my own publisher at BMG later that afternoon, I had almost the same experience: grown men and women tearing up as they talked about their children.

By four o'clock I put in a call to Peter, explaining what had happened that morning, including the mysterious voice I had heard, and the events throughout the day. "I think I want to have a baby," I said tentatively.

"Wow, I can't believe it! I'm in shock but . . . I think it's great!" Peter replied.

"Yeah, me, too. Do you think my age has anything to do with me feeling this way?" I wondered aloud. "I mean, I'm thirty-four. Do you think my biological clock has gone off?"

He laughed, "I don't think biological clocks have voices."

That night we said a prayer before dinner, thanking God for the events of the day. Afterward Peter said, "Boy, this has really been a red-letter day." When he said that, something inside me clicked.

"What's the date?" I asked.

"Uh . . . June thirtieth."

"You know," I said, "I'm not sure . . . but I think today is my mother's birthday. I'm going to go call Dad and find out."

Dad confirmed for me that it was, indeed, my mother's birthday. I decided to tell him the news. Not surprisingly, he laughed. "I'll believe *that* when I see it," he said.

It took almost six months before we got a little plus sign on our pregnancy indicator. We were so excited. The day was January seventh, my Dad's birthday, so we decided to call and give him the good news.

We sang the birthday song to him, ending it with "Happy Birthday, dear Grampa . . . Happy Birthday to you." He was pretty excited, too, and immediately asked when the baby would be due.

"September seventh," I answered.

He took an audible breath as if he were surprised. "That's the day your mother died," he said reverently.

Piecing together all the events leading up to my pregnancy and knowing that there was some kind of link to my mother gave me an incredible sense of peace. I really felt I was in God's perfect will—everything was in His hands.

The pregnancy went along very smoothly with both of us in suspense about who our little one would be. For some reason, perhaps some old wives' tale about how I was carrying the baby, we fell under the assumption that our child would be a boy. We had his name picked out—he would be Houstin, after Peter's father.

Ignoring its own due date (as babies usually do), our child arrived on the eleventh of September and surprised us all by being a beautiful little girl. As any parent knows, it was a blessed day for us; and having a girl granted me my lifetime wish of having a mother/daughter relationship— only now I would be the mother.

We named her Christina Leigh, and the day after she was born Peter came into the hospital room with some news: "Stowe," he said, his eyes wide with excitement. "There's a little baby with the last name of Biter lying in a crib next to Christina. Do you think she's related to your mother?"

I thought about it a moment. Though I had never met any of my mother's family (they all died before I was born), I was pretty sure they came from somewhere north of Nashville. I looked at Peter. "Is it spelled like my mother's last name? B-I-T-E-R?"

"Yep."

"Wow. I would think they'd *have* to be related."

So as soon as I was able, I headed down the hall to the Biter room. The young man who greeted me said his name was James (just like my grandfather). In the next few weeks he introduced us to his grandfather, who knew mine and was able to relate some stories about the family I never knew. What a joy it was to connect with these long-lost relatives. And what an inspiring journey it was on my path to parenthood.

I absolutely love being a mother—in fact, it feels like the most natural thing in the world for me. It goes without

saying that it hasn't all been a joyride; but on those difficult days when life seems hard, I find comfort in looking
back to the beginning of this story.

I'm convinced that by stepping out in faith and not hiding behind my fears and doubts, I was able to follow that
small voice (which I believe was sent from God) to exactly
where I needed to be. And because of this it wasn't long
before I was telling Peter again, "I want to have another
baby."

Twenty-three months later Grace Caroline was born—
a little sister for Christina. Our nest felt full and I felt
grounded, with solid reasons to pursue healthy and loving
family relationships—far different from the dysfunctional
and disconnected way in which I was raised.

I knew I was still in the fight, and every day was a battle, but I finally made the link between my connectedness
with God and my connectedness with the rest of the world.
I was discovering, through experience, that I had the
strength to forge ahead and find all the disconnections that
stood in the way of perfect union with God and the people
I loved most.

✦

Peter
Back in college, I read a great deal about a relatively new area
of neurobiology called split-brain studies.

THE SCIENTIFIC APPROACH
TO TEAMWORK

Roger Sperry won a Nobel Prize in 1981 for his groundbreaking research into the functions of the left and right hemispheres of the brain in epileptic patients. By cutting the corpus callosum—the thick bundle of nerve fibers that link the two sides of the brain—in order to control severe seizures, Sperry observed dramatic differences in functional skills between the disconnected halves. His findings indicated that the left side of our brain specializes in verbal, logical, linear thinking, whereas the right brain focuses on more spatial, intuitive, and creative reasoning. This led to a tidal wave of theories in pop psychology, philosophy, and even spirituality . . . some going as far as to suggest that the right hemisphere of the brain is where the spirit resides.[1]

After twenty years of left-right caricatures, in which motivational speakers called for submissive right brains to declare independence from overbearing left brains, scientists are now saying our brains are not so simplistic as all that. In my own layman's understanding of the newest findings, both sides of the brain are capable of functioning in ways that cross the boundaries of simple left-does-the-talking, right-does-the-art definitions.

Joseph Hellige, a psychologist at the University of Southern California, used electromagnetic brain-scanning experiments that showed various sections of the brain lighting up on a display monitor when patients were subjected to various stimuli, ranging from language questions to spatial awareness tests. Rather than proving that the left side of the brain exclusively handles language and the right side deals exclusively with spatial challenges, as commonly portrayed, it seemed to show that *subtle processing styles* distinguished the two halves. For example, when stimulated by language tests, the left hemisphere lit up if specifically challenged with grammar, whereas the right side lit up when challenged by intonation.[2]

Yes, there may be a difference in their bias, but each side is called upon to contribute its own viewpoint on any given situation. Bottom line: The two halves of our brain are designed to work together, the same input processed from two different perspectives. Our mental faculties for processing the world are shared in a rapid-fire exchange of information between the two halves, each side contributing in a complementary way, but not competitively or exclusively.

A smart brain is not dominated by either the left or right hemisphere; it can process both the *details* and the *big picture* at once—in other words, a smart brain experiences respectful teamwork.

FOLLOWING GOD'S MODEL FOR THE DREAM TEAM

Now, I like that model of our God-given computer a lot better than the dominant/submissive relationship that seemed more likely to have conflicts with itself and crash like my PC. And it speaks to my heart, once again, about the importance of recognizing the natural connections inherent in our design. The symmetry and balance between the two halves of our brain says volumes about how God intended us to work with other people, too. When two or more work together as an effective team, the same mutually respectful and complementary attitudes come into play as are found in a "smart brain."

I have been so blessed to share many wonderful partnerships and collaborations with a great number of coworkers. The best of those relationships involved attitudes of mutual admiration for each other's skills and shared respect for one another's opinions. If those attitudes aren't shared, the relationship doesn't last long.

The greatest partnership I have ever experienced, by far, is with my wife Stowe. She and I have shared so many joint ventures I can hardly name them all: books, films, songs, houses, landscaping, gardening, decorating, cooking, child-raising . . . the list goes on forever. And what makes our partnership work is a strong sense of connection, built upon mutual respect and lots of communication. Just like the rapid-fire exchange between the left and right hemispheres of the brain, we are constantly talking about our different viewpoints of the tasks at hand.

Often we see things *very* differently, but we are both careful not to dominate or criticize one another in a way that would disconnect our spiritual link. Our marriage, like any good marriage, is a spiritual union—our spirits are merged as one. I recognize God's own Spirit that He breathed into Stowe, and I trust she will find the same in me.

We've seen this principle work successfully for us again and again. When we bat ideas around until we both genuinely like the game plan, then the project turns out wonderfully. Building on the success of mutual honor and respect, we've shared a great life together. And with that kind of open channel of communication, where we each feel safe to talk about our hopes and dreams, we've seen a great number of our dreams come true. After all, we are *The Dream Team*. When the shoe fits . . .

ALFRED AND EVELYN BENNETT

We met another "dream team" on a beautiful Sunday several autumns ago. Stowe and I were visiting the little antique district of charming downtown Nolensville, Tennessee. Nestled between the antique stores and the old-time feed mill was a cute little bed-and-breakfast named The Homeplace. It had an old-style front porch with rocking chairs, and the whole house was surrounded by beautiful gardens.

I had wanted to go inside The Homeplace several times because Stowe and I had occasionally dreamed about owning a B&B of our own someday.

On this particular Sunday, while perusing inside a little antique shop across the street from The Homeplace, I noticed through the shop window that the B&B's proprietor was outside, blowing leaves off the sidewalk. So, as Stowe lingered over antiques, I walked over to meet the dignified gentleman who appeared to be in his late sixties or early seventies. I was immediately greeted by a warm handshake and friendly smile as we exchanged names. Alfred Bennett caught me off guard when he said, "Well, you must be my appointment today. . . . I've been waiting for you."

"Oh, no. I'm afraid not. . . ." I replied. "I just dropped by unannounced because my wife and I have been curious to see your place."

"Well, then you *are* my appointment!" he said with a warm expression in his eyes. "You see, I believe God sets up an appointment for me every day to meet someone new, whom I'm supposed to learn something from. Today, I was meant to meet you!"

About that time Stowe strolled up with our girls and I

made more introductions. Soon we were inside The Home-place, tempted by the offer of lemonade, tea, and cookies. Al-fred introduced us to his lovely wife, Evelyn Bennett, whose gracious smile was the perfect counterpart to his own. Evelyn got around in an electric wheelchair, on account of polio she contracted as a child.

As Stowe and the girls visited with Evelyn, I joined Alfred on a tour of his gardens, which inspired my own budding green thumb. I learned that Alfred was a retired Presbyterian minister and had once served a congregation in New Orleans. This gave a clue to the inspiration for his beautiful courtyard gardens, reminiscent of those found in the French Quarter. It also explained Alfred's ripe spiritual wisdom, which I would soon begin to receive. He then took me to the back of the property to see another treasure—a pair of rustic, small Vic-torian barns set beside a creek whose current had once pow-ered the neighboring feed mill. One of the barns was for storage and the other was set up as an open-air sitting room that overlooked the creek.

"This creek house is where I come to do my best meditat-ing," explained Mr. Bennett. "Even though I can no longer see with my eyes, I can come down here and commune with my Maker."

"What do you mean you can't see with your eyes?" I asked, puzzled by what my tour guide said. I then discovered that Al-fred is "blind as a bat," due to macular degeneration, which leaves him seeing only faint shadows of light and dark around his peripheral vision. It came as a shock because Alfred seemed to have a gift of looking straight into my soul while making direct eye contact.

As we sat in the creek house talking about life, God's love, and the Holy Spirit—while scorning all kinds of religious hypocrisy—something dawned on me. Here is an older married couple who enjoy life to the fullest, while one is blind and the other can't walk . . . and they run a B&B with all the grace and hospitality of people in their prime! I had to know more about what gave them such energy and determination. And, preacher that he is, Alfred was more than willing to share his secret of a happy marriage with me.

"You see," Alfred began, "I have discovered that each of us is made up of two halves . . . beginning when we are first conceived. When the half of you that comes from your father's seed joins the half that is from your mother, your cells begin dividing symmetrically."

I blinked and nodded, not knowing quite how basic this philosophy might get.

"We each have a male side and a female side," he continued. "With qualities passed down from our mother and father, who in turn inherited qualities from their own mothers and fathers."

"Okay . . ." I said, still waiting to hear how this related to a happy marriage.

"So, until we each recognize that we contain both female and male character qualities, we can't be fully balanced as individuals. And unless a marriage is composed of two balanced people, it'll run through life like a wobbly wheel."

Now I started connecting to what he was saying. I, too, have found wisdom in recognizing my own contrasting male and female qualities; a nurturing side and an aggressive side; simultaneously intuitive and logical; both emotional and calculating, and so on. I know that I have inherited both the logical business skills of my lawyer father and the creative talents of my artist mother. Sometimes I enjoy doing computer spreadsheets. Sometimes I enjoy cooking. This shouldn't be mistaken for stereotyped gender roles, where women do only women's work and men do just manly things. On the contrary, an individual who understands it is not just okay, but extremely wise to balance one's own male and female halves and is much more likely to have a happy and peaceful marriage with someone else who is also evenly balanced. Again, I am reminded of the left and right brain, working as two halves of a whole but with *subtle differences in operating styles.*

Alfred and Evelyn Bennett have found that wonderful harmony in their lives. Evelyn is every bit a southern lady—both she and her home are brimming with style—but she has no trouble doing the books for their business. And Alfred is just as likely to be found tending his garden with artistic sensitivity as he would be building a rock wall, doing trim carpentry, or composing a clever sermon. He is locally famous for sporting the Wallace tartan, and if any man ever doubts his own masculinity, try wearing a kilt in public . . . it'll bring out the male swagger in any guy. I know this from personal experience because Alfred dared me, and I have pictures to prove it!

"If people deny the opposite-sex qualities in themselves, they are simply disconnected from half of their own inheritance," added Alfred.

"Think about the inner relationship of your male and female characteristics as a happy marriage. If you think of your male side as the valiant hunter, and the female side as the intuitive nurturer, then consider what a wonderful partnership you have within yourself. The female side respectfully says, 'We need food,' or 'We need money,' or 'We need a place to rest,' and the loving male side replies, 'Absolutely, my dear. . . . I'll go get it.' Together, our two halves possess all the qualities

God intended for us to be able to survive in this world, intuitively and compassionately feeling what is needed, and then aggressively and logically figuring out how to get it. But—and this is the key—like a happy marriage, we must submit ourselves to God's will . . . to be guided by His Spirit."[3]

Ideally, *healthy connections* are what all these things share in common . . . whether talking about a husband and wife; our inner male and female qualities; or our left and right brains. We function better when our different halves get along. And, I believe, they work best when all the parts are connected by the love of the One who designed us in the first place.

Stowe

Wouldn't we all love to believe we can stand up to the fiercest storms and still keep our healthy connections intact? When life is good and everything is going my way, it's easy for me to say, "Yes, I trust You, Lord, and I'm going to follow You into the eye of the hurricane—no questions asked." But then reality steps in and reminds me of how imperfect I am. I'm the first to admit that when the storm hits, I tend to run for cover.

As Peter mentioned earlier, we often find ourselves facing financial hurdles in our marriage—times when we don't quite have enough money to pay the piper. We've always worked for royalities, and while some months are abundant, more often than not we go for long spells with little or no income. This, of course, is a hard position to be in, and during those times we cling to one another and to our faith that God will provide for our needs—as He always has.

I must admit, though, back in the early days there were many moments when I faltered, wondering out loud with teary eyes, *How are we going to make the next mortgage payment?* It was always Peter who took my hand in his and, closing his eyes, boldly thanked the Lord for taking care of our every need. Peter's grateful heart was never ignored. I cannot begin to count the times when unexpected checks—for just the right amount of money—made their way into our mailbox, or when freelance jobs seemed to drop out of the sky. Peter has taught me a lot in the department of faithfulness, and over the years my faith has blossomed.

"KEEP GOING. LOVE, GOD"

Let me take you back to that moment, though, when Peter needed some strong encouragement. For months he had been working diligently, proposing different film projects. But over and over, his ideas were rejected. Our quickly dwindling savings and the lack of prospective work was finally getting to him; Peter wanted nothing more than to be a good husband and provide security.

One afternoon I found him lying on the bed instead of working in his office. This was very unusual, and I went to his side. The look on his face was one of utter defeat, and he shared with me his concern about whether or not he was pursuing the right career path. Having had little success recently with inspirational films, he was beginning to question if this was truly what God wanted him to do. Then he turned and looked up at me. "If only God would give me a sign . . ." he said. Tears welled in his eyes. "A sign that I'm on the right path."

Suddenly it seemed as if God were whispering to me. I jumped up and hurried into my office. Acting on what I felt was an inspiration from God, I grabbed a pen, a scrap of paper, and said a quick prayer. Then I wrote what I felt in my heart was a message Peter needed to hear.

I believed in my husband's work. I believed he should continue, and I knew God did, too. I took the paper back into the bedroom and gave it to him. He read the words out loud. "You're on the right path. Keep going. Love, God."

"It's a special sign for you," I beamed.

Peter told me, much later, that it wasn't so much the paper sign that spoke to him, but the underlying message of our partnership—that I was okay with the journey we were on together. I know the Lord inspired that message, and my confirmation gave Peter the sign he needed.

Just a few days later we got the good news that one of my songs, "Long Time Comin'," had been chosen as the title cut on the latest Shenandoah album. We were thrilled, and even more so when we found out I would be able to get an advance on my royalties. That bit of income was enough to hold us over until Peter got news from the Learning Channel that they were ready to give the green light to his program, *Angel Stories*. That, in turn, cleared the way for six more years of related programming about miracles, angels, and the afterlife. All these events were a clear and wonderful sign to us.

I'm not sure if those words ("You're on the right path. Keep going. Love, God.") meant more that day or in the many subsequent years since we taped it to our bedroom mirror. On a daily basis I seldom see it, and months can go by without it catching my attention. Yet, whenever I'm questioning if what we are doing together is right, those words always seem to find me.

As long as we continue to pray and remain in communication with God, we can keep going, feeling assured we are indeed on the right path together. It is one of the most important lessons we have learned: When God inspires a direction, He also prepares a way. Even though we don't dwell in the past, we never forget what lies behind us; and if there's unfinished business back there, we have to face it before we can move ahead.

CHAPTER TWELVE

AN OPEN DOOR TO
THE PAST

Then your light will shine like the dawning sun,
and you will quickly be healed. Your honesty will
protect you as you advance, and the glory of the
LORD will defend you from behind.

—ISAIAH 58:8 CEV

Stowe's Journey

In 1998, after the girls were born, my father decided to move to Nashville—to be closer to us. Living within fifteen minutes of one another was a mixed blessing— we made some fun memories, but with all the baggage from our past and with alcohol still very much a part of my father's life, there were also plenty of stressful times. Still, it was a time for learning to be more open and honest with each other—something we sorely needed to do.

Some of the things my father shared with me, however, were a little hard to swallow. For instance, when we dis- cussed his thoughts about dying, he told me he wanted to die in our home surrounded by his family, *Okay . . . I guess I could accept that.*

But then he began to go on about what he expected from me: I was his daughter, therefore he wanted me to "be his servant" (his own words) during his final days. He expected me to wait on him and take care of him. Never mind that I had a husband and two young children! As far as he was concerned, that's the way it would be—end of conversation.

I swallowed hard as I felt my stomach tighten. I wanted to honor my father, but knowing how controlling he could be was causing quite a stressful feeling within my soul. Still, I didn't say anything . . . anyway, who knew how or when the end would come?

But it seemed that no sooner than we had this conversa-tion, Dad got the call about his cancer. Suddenly, being the caretaker of the one who had not taken care of me looked quite imminent. The fear within me was palpable. So it seemed no mere coincidence that my dream about being an abused child was my subconscious way of bringing to the surface the poisonous memories that had been stored in my mind and body for so long.

But *knowing* it was time to come face-to-face with my past, and *actually doing* anything about it, were different matters. I wanted to holler, *Please don't make me go back there again. . . . It hurts too much.* Still, I didn't cry out or say anything to anyone. I continued on my usual path and held my thoughts and feelings inside—just like old times. For me, holding things inside equals depression, and that was the state I was in one week after my fateful dream.

✳

Peter
Perhaps it was God's way of preparing us for the idea of "heal-ing" traumatic memories, because the following incident opened our hearts and minds to allow just that.

In an episode of *Miracles, Angels & Afterlife* we focused on reports of miraculous healings, particularly by the laying on of hands. I must confess that, in the interest of good television, we sought out what seemed to be the most dramatic cases of healings, in hopes that we might be able to document a miracle in progress. We interviewed a woman named Sharon, who claims to have performed instantaneous healing through physical touch for many years.

We asked Sharon to show us exactly what she does, and we offered to conduct an impromptu workshop in our home. She agreed, so we invited several friends and neighbors to participate in the event.

After a brief introduction from Sharon on what we were going to do, we broke into pairs and took turns performing Sharon's healing methods on each other. No one in the room claimed to have any particular afflictions, so the prayer was simple: *If there is anything in need of healing that we aren't aware of, please address it.*

We then did some deep-breathing exercises to help focus our attention on the areas in need of addressing. It was a very relaxing experience for me, but several people around the room became quietly emotional. One woman in particular underwent a profound healing experience that brought her face-to-face with her past—a horrible experience she didn't recall until this moment.

LINDA

"Linda" is a close friend of ours. She is a registered nurse and a busy massage therapist. During our workshop she was paired with my associate producer, Fred Rowles. Fred had himself experienced miraculous healing on past occasions. As Fred held his hands on Linda's head, she relaxed to the floor. After a while she began weeping. And then her cries grew louder.

I was across the room, also on the floor, so I didn't see what was happening, but I could clearly hear that Linda was very disturbed by something. She later described in a taped interview what she experienced:

"When the hands were placed on me, I wasn't sure what would happen. Then, the next thing I knew, I was in a state of not being totally unconscious, but not being entirely conscious, either. I went back to a time when I was five years old and in a neighbor's garage." (I should add that before the session began, Sharon had explained that sometimes a person may revert back to a memory from long ago.)

Linda continued, "I had totally blocked out this experience for the past thirty-five years. I had no recollection until this healing session that it had even occurred. It was sexual abuse. . . . I was made to perform acts that I did not want to perform."

During the session, I heard Linda say, "No . . . no . . . no . . . You are a bad boy, Jimmy. . . ." And then she sobbed loudly while crying out, "I'm not a bad girl . . . and you are a very, very bad boy!"

When I interviewed her later, Linda recalled the years that followed the sexual assault by the teenage neighbor. "Several years afterward, when I was ten years old, my mother had taken me to a doctor for an upper GI because I was having difficulty swallowing. . . . I can remember feeling that way my whole life, even until recently. A year or two ago, I went to a doctor and just felt like there was a tumor in my throat or maybe my thyroid was enlarged or something that was preventing me from swallowing. I now realize that it stems back to when I was five years old in that garage, where I was forced to swallow something that I didn't want to."

There was something else that happened with Linda during the session, and I still don't know what to make of it. Several people in the workshop smelled an intense scent of cat urine, which was totally foreign to our house because neither our neighbors nor we have had cats.

Fred Rowles, Linda's partner in the workshop, described the scene from his perspective:

"Sharon had told us that sometimes there are odors associated with this process as the body is getting rid of toxins, and I started to smell something—it smelled like cat urine, and it came up at two distinct times when Linda was in her most severe pain."

Later, we found out from Linda that she had indeed been assaulted in a garage where cats were kept.

Fred also remembered another detail from the healing session. "I remember at one point Linda taking my hand and moving it over her own eyes, and I had no idea why she was doing that. I thought she was trying to shield herself from seeing what was going on in the garage."

As Linda remembered it, "During the experience I kept seeing a bright light and thinking that it was the camera crew and their lights. It was just a blinding, blinding light. And after the experience, talking to Sharon, she made me aware that there were no camera lights near me at the time, and she felt it may have been the light of God there with me. . . . I think I felt that, too, at the time. I felt very safe. I felt I was not going to be harmed, and it was just a very comforting experience to know God was there with me."

Nearly two years after the workshop, I asked Linda if the experience had any lasting effect on her life. She told me it had, in fact, liberated her from a long history of feeling sexually powerless. She said she had always felt victimized and that sexual advances by men were beyond her control . . . but no more. Further, she explained this was not only a life-changing experience, "but probably a life-prolonging experience, because I believe if this memory had been left there without coming to the surface and my being able to deal with it, I probably would have manifested some kind of real disease."[1]

HEALING IS MORE THAN JUST SURVIVING

Almost everyone has past traumas, whether hidden or easily recalled. If we manage our past the way Stowe and Linda managed theirs—by pushing it down into our subconscious and ignoring the pain we feel—we may find ourselves frequently in the position of powerless victim, constantly at the mercy of our emotions and inability to handle conflicts in relationships. We may not be able to pursue the dreams and passions of our lives. We may shy from connecting with people—and with God—because we're afraid, without even knowing it sometimes, of being hurt or shamed.

Pain from the past, however, is very personal, and every person is different in how they interpret their level of pain and how they deal with their grief. Whereas one person may be able to successfully manage the pain of a divorce and move on with a healthy life, another person may drag the same experience behind them like a heavy suitcase laden with shame and resentment. In stark contrast, one person may handle severe child abuse much easier than another person might handle being stood up by a date on homecoming night.

The stages of grief are individually variable, and the time involved in navigating each stage is even more unpredictable; so the goal, of course, is to be careful not to minimize another person's pain. Healing can take place only in a safe environment where the hard, thorny outer layers of the past can be carefully peeled away to reveal a soft and pliable center that God can mold into His own image, by the warmth of his own loving Light.

PART III

RECONNECTING
TO THE LIGHT

CHAPTER THIRTEEN

HEALING REVELATIONS

*But to each one is given the manifestation of the
Spirit for the common good. For to one is given the
word of wisdom through the Spirit, and to another
the word of knowledge according to the same Spirit;
to another faith by the same Spirit, and to another
gifts of healing by the one Spirit, and to another the
effecting of miracles, and to another prophecy, and
to another the distinguishing of spirits, to another
various kinds of tongues, and to another the
interpretation of tongues. But one and the same
Spirit works all these things, distributing to each
one individually just as He wills.*

—1 COR. 12:7–11 NASB

Stowe's Journey

During the week following my dream, I was in a
state of worsening depression. Peter was working
in the yard when I once again heard the phone
ringing. I didn't feel like talking to anyone, so I let it ring.
Then a moment later my mobile phone rang. I assumed it
must be a family member trying to reach us, so I answered
it. But it wasn't family—it was a lady named Jean Bertram.
I was barely listening as Ms. Bertram explained how she
had talked to my husband the previous week, and now she

wanted to come by for a visit to talk about one of our upcoming projects.

"I'm visiting Nashville today, and I could come by in about an hour," she said. "Would that be okay?" I rolled my eyes; the last thing I wanted was company.

"Uh . . . well, I'll go talk to my husband," I said softly. "Hold on." I walked outside and told Peter about the call. He was more than happy to have her come over. I was outnumbered. Within thirty minutes Jean was knocking on our door.

She was a friendly, talkative woman, and it took her only a few minutes to open up to us and begin sharing her life story—she, too, had been a victim of child abuse, and that part of her story resonated strongly with me. We were quite mesmerized by Jean and spent the rest of the day asking questions and listening to her.

At one point in our meeting Jean looked at me and casually pointed to the rash on my hands—the one that appeared after my dream that resurfaced hidden memories of child abuse. She said, "That rash will go away if you rebuke it."

Caught off guard by her remarks, I stammered, "Rebuke it?"

"Mm-hmm," she said, nodding confidently. "You just need to rebuke it in the name of Jesus. Don't allow it in your life." She then continued on with her story while I pondered her remarks.

Rebuke it in the name of Jesus. . . . She made it sound as if demons had taken hold of me. But the more I thought about it, the more I thought she may be right. Could an "unclean spirit," as Jesus called them, cause such depression in me? Surely God would never wish that on anyone. I felt that

Jean was telling me to stop being a victim—to take charge and ask God to intervene; but I was still a little shaky in that department. What if nothing happened? What if I prayed and God didn't move?

Later that afternoon as Jean was preparing to leave, Peter asked her if she would pray with me for the healing of my terrible rash, and she was more than happy to oblige.

First I told her about my dream. She interpreted the other woman in the dream to be a reflection of myself—the lost, dejected, and somewhat angry side of me. I asked her about the writing on my arm. *Why was it white?* She smiled and lovingly said, "That's so you'll know it's a message from God—it's pure and white."

Facing me, Jean took my hands in hers and began a simple, sweet, and sincere prayer. It felt good to have her pray for me, but I must admit I was skeptical; I didn't hold out much hope of opening my eyes and seeing the rash gone. Sure enough, when she was finished praying, the rash was still there. But I thanked her anyway, and Peter and I walked her to the door to say our good-byes.

While she and Peter talked a little more, I absentmindedly put my hands together and something caught my attention. My hands—they didn't itch! I rubbed my hands together to make sure. For the first time in a week there was no sensation of itching. Excited, I broke into their conversation. "Jean! My hands! They've stopped itching!" She immediately looked toward heaven and gave a big "Hallelujah," then danced a little jig. I suddenly felt rejuvenated with hope, and I was truly grateful for this new feeling. Over the next few days I watched in wonder as the rash quickly disappeared. God had actually performed a miracle—on *me*—though I feel pretty sure it was not the first miracle God has worked in my life, it was one I could actually see at that moment. But the most amazing thing has been the miracle occurring within my spirit. It didn't happen overnight, nor has it been without work or pain, but I started to feel like a new woman.

Within a week of Jean's visit, I began a new chapter in my life—one on healing the inner wounds. With Jean's encouragement I started writing the story of my own journey—the one you are reading now. It wasn't an easy thing to do. More than once I dreaded writing a particular part of this, and there were many times when our girls came running into my office asking me, "Mama, why are you crying?" But with each tear shed, the burden I had carried for so long on my own became lighter. I can't tell you how relieved I feel to have literally gotten this off my chest.

Peter
So who is Jean Bertram? And how did this remarkable woman discover her mile marker on the journeys of so many hurting people?

JEAN BERTRAM

Jean Bertram is a woman who enjoys spending a great deal of time in prayer, often going out to a secluded area for hours at a time in order to be alone with God. She also loves studying the Bible. Several years ago Jean read something in the New

Testament that caught her attention. Though she had read it many times before, on this particular occasion it spoke directly to her heart. "Each time Jesus performs the miracle of healing," she recalls, "the Bible says 'and he was moved with compassion.' *Compassion* was the factor that moved him to *pray for healing*." Jean understood this kind of compassion, for she considered herself to be a very sympathetic woman, and she often felt moved to pray for people.

Once, when Jean heard about a woman whose husband had died, she felt moved to bring the woman dinner. The woman was surprised to see Jean and wondered how Jean even knew about her husband's death, since the two ladies had never met and didn't appear to have any common acquaintances. Nonetheless, the woman was grateful to receive the dinner Jean made because guests were coming, and there wasn't nearly enough food to feed them and the woman's family.

"She was feeling lost and alone," Jean says, "but she saw how God made a way for her guests and children to eat that night." With a big smile Jean says, "To me, that is so awesome. . . . God's love moves people and lets them know, 'Yes, you do matter.' Nothing changes unless someone is moved to compassion."

By showing compassion for our fellow man, we connect ourselves to one another and to God. "We have the ability to make a perfect balance for each other," Jean says, "but we all have to do our part." Jean's own part in the journey begins with one of her greatest gifts: compassion. "My favorite thing to do is lay my hands on people because there are so many who need it. Everybody is looking for the same thing—for someone to look at them and say, 'You matter . . . God loves you . . . you're important.' All things grow with love, and I've learned there are all kinds of healing—not just the physical kind."

Jean says, "God is in charge, and He knows exactly what He's doing. . . . All I have to do is show up; He takes care of the rest. He calms my fears, and He calms others' fears. I see the strength He gives people . . . and it's all good. So it's been the best thing in my life—it's what I love to do most—when I'm called to pray for people."

Over time, Jean has become much more secure in her role as a healer. She says, "The thing I love about healing is that it gives me the opportunity to see the Spirit move and to see the power of love. As I've gotten older, I would welcome the hordes at the door because that's the greatest thing to me—to just spread that love. And I do it every chance I get!"[1]

Stowe

Not long after meeting Jean Bertram, I began daydreaming about what it would be like to have the gift of healing—of letting God's spirit work through me. *Wouldn't it be wonderful*, I thought, *if I could help people in that way—laying hands on people who need it most and being instrumental in healing their bodies and minds?*

To do this I would need to pray for the gift of healing, and I was not yet sure it was my calling.

A GIFT OR A BURDEN?

Before going into deep prayer to request this gift, I decided to consult with Jean. Her response to me was surprising. "This gift is a heavy burden to bear," Jean earnestly replied. "I've had it since I was a child and I love it; some days it's absolutely wonderful. But I'll be honest with you. There are a lot of other times when it just breaks my heart." She ended by saying, "You should really pray about whether this is God's plan for you . . . I'll even pray about it, too."

So I prayed about it, and I thought about it. And I came to the conclusion that it was not my full-time calling to lay hands on the sick. Yes, I will do it when someone asks; but from what I read in 1 Cor. 12:7–11, healing is a special gift from the Holy Spirit, which a person is called *specifically* to bear. Still, I kept wishing there was something I could do to help those whom I knew were suffering.

Jean called me back a few days later and said, after praying, that she felt strongly that God had given me the gift of *exhortation*, and that my writing, too, could be useful to others. She felt, however, that before I could move in that direction, I would first need to seek my own healing. Writing my life story, she said, would help enable me do that.

I agreed that reviewing my life would probably be good for me. I wasn't so sure, though, about being an adviser to others or even *helping* people with my writing. But I thanked her for her prayers and said I would think about it.

Reviewing one's life and actually facing the suppressed shadows of one's past are two very different things. To tell the truth, I wasn't entirely ready to do either; but God had my course charted, and my present and future were about to collide with my past for one final showdown.

CHAPTER FOURTEEN

CROSSING THE BITTER BRIDGE

*For there is a proper time and procedure for every
delight, though a man's trouble is heavy upon him.
If no one knows what will happen, who
can tell him when it will happen?*

—ECCLES. 8:6–7 NASB

Stowe's Journey

Overcoming the terrible rash that invaded my body was the first step in repairing the broken connections of my life. But there was something else I had to do: I shared with my dying father the dream, praying that it might somehow connect us a little more. It wasn't easy for me to tell it, or for him to hear it. I'm not even sure he even "got it," but the important thing for me was that I had the courage to tell him. Before the dream and the healing of my heart and hands, I wouldn't have had the nerve to tell him about anything so personal and spiritual in nature.

It was January 2001, about eight months after my dream, when Dad came to visit. He seemed nervous and, standing in front of me, took my hand and placed it on the side of his neck. I felt my stomach drop as I touched three hard lumps that ran along his lymph glands. "The doctor says I have three, maybe six months left, honey."

As usual, Dad had many lists of things he and I needed to do for him—this time to prepare for his death. We diligently did everything he ordered, and his attitude was positive for the most part. It had been a couple of months since his first round of chemo treatments and he was beginning to look and feel better—several of our outings were sprinkled with some of the old humor. *I cherish those memories.*

The following week, I took him for the beginning of his second round of chemo treatments. I thought he handled it well, but several days later he came down with a cold. As sick as he was, the doctors didn't seem too concerned— they just prescribed over-the-counter cold medicine. Still, nothing really helped him feel better, and he was often short-tempered with me. One of the side effects of my recent healing was a newfound desire to stand up for myself, so we were clashing a lot more.

On Friday, February fourth, he called and said he would like to come and stay with us. Deep inside I feared he might be coming to live with us—probably for many months! Even though he could hardly speak (he had a temporary condition known as thrush), he still took charge of every detail. Scribbling on small pieces of paper, he dictated to us everything he wanted from his apartment. He didn't overlook slipping a small bottle of alcohol into his bag.

At home, our guestroom was immediately rearranged and rendered unrecognizable, and a bell was set up by his bedside so he could summon me.

Inside my soul I was screaming, *He's taking over my life!*

I was overwhelmed with feelings of helplessness, and I was in constant need of a tissue. I tried so hard to hide the tears—I didn't want to make Dad feel bad, and I really didn't want to upset the girls, but it was useless. This was not a healthy pouring out of my feelings—it was more like a leaky faucet with a constant trickle. Even after all the healing I had experienced, here I was still bottling up my feelings—just as I had learned to do so well all my life. And I couldn't admit this to anyone—not even to myself.

The next morning I awoke to the sound of Dad ringing his bell. It was 6:00 A.M. I stumbled down the hall to find my father perched on the side of his bed, pointing authoritatively to a note he had just written: *Go to the store and get me some juice and aspirin.* Even though he could barely talk, we somehow managed to have a small argument, perhaps about his handwriting, which was illegible. Giving him a tight-lipped smile, I set off on my errand, feeling resentful about my appointed task. Once arriving at the store, I wandered the aisles, sobbing uncontrollably. I couldn't hold it in any longer.

Yes, I was in a very self-centered place—all I could imagine was what hell my life was going to be over the coming months. I hate to say it, but I had almost no sympathy for my ill father. Upon returning home, however, he thanked me and stared up at my red, swollen eyes as if to say, *What's wrong with you? Why can't you pull yourself together?* Finally, he shook his head and, in a sarcastic whisper, said, "Cheer up."

I forced a little smile. "I'll try."

Dad stayed in bed most of that day; Peter and I occasionally checked on him. His cough and stuffiness seemed be getting worse, and in the afternoon we called his doctor for advice. The nurse didn't seem concerned and suggested more cold medicine and bed rest.

I went into his room once that evening and attempted to make pleasant conversation. It was going well until the girls came in to say hello. Rather gruffly, he asked them to leave, and then criticized my handling of them. Resentful and angry, I left the room. *I can't see how any of us can go on in this way for an extended period of time.*

Peter, on the other hand, didn't carry all the baggage of the parent/child relationship, so he was willing and able to care for my father in a loving manner. Sensing that I couldn't do anything more for Dad that evening, Peter felt inspired to gently wash and put lotion on Dad's poor old feet—a treatment I'm sure Dad enjoyed. Peter then helped him back into bed. But shortly afterward, Peter noticed Dad having difficulty with his breathing, and his eyes seemed to be unfocused.

I was reading a bedtime story to the girls when Peter came to me with a serious look on his face. Leading me into the hallway, he whispered, "Stowe, I think it's the end."

"What?" I couldn't believe what I was hearing. "What are you talking about?"

"He's hardly breathing."

I stared at him. *Surely you're imagining things,* I thought. *He has cancer and a cold . . . but he's not dying!* Snapping to attention, I went quickly to Dad's bedside. One look at him slumped over on the bed told me Peter was right. He was still breathing, though just barely. Taking his hand, I tried to bring him around. "Dad . . . Dad . . ."

It was too late.

A few agonizing moments later—after living in our

home for less than a day—my father took his last breath. Peter and I sat beside his body for the next hour or so, holding his hands and—between our tears—praying for him, encouraging him to go toward the Light.

✦

Peter
There is a fine line between the emotional and the logical aspects of death. Where we are in the equation—how attached we were to the departed life—dictates how emotional or how practical we are about the death.

THE OTHER SIDE OF MISERY

We humans tend to put a shortsighted emphasis on our earthly life (in the eternal scheme of things), and some of us consider death to be the ultimate *negative* scenario; that no good can come from it. But from what I understand, after my studies into near-death experiences, dying is not something to be feared like some dark alley—and neither is life. Grief for a deceased loved one is a natural and normal reaction to a lost relationship, but unresolved grief can turn into anger, bitterness, and frustration. Sure, it's simple to put the practical mind-set into action—in theory, in the setting of a practicum. But the death of Stowe's father proved to us, once again, that life isn't lived in a fishbowl. Saying her final farewell to a man who has been a part of her entire life—even though this person may have unwittingly injured her—was an emotionally draining and devastatingly painful event for my wife.

Earlier I pointed out that many of life's worst scenarios

have become catalysts for positive change. Every event has a ripple effect on the rest of the world for the rest of time. Tragic deaths have resulted in many tears, yes; but we cannot ignore the immeasurable healing that can take place through the grieving process. As undesirable and painful as divorce is, it is possible that the trauma of divorce can bring healing in hidden areas that are brought to light only through the loss of the relationship. Losing your job is devastating, but it can bring new opportunities, open new doors, create new relationships, and lead to soaring heights that couldn't be seen nor imagined from your previous place on the ground.

Sometimes there is no "bright side" to a tragic event; sometimes bad things happen and we just feel terrible for a long time. But faith-centered grieving can open the door to new life. And I certainly don't mean simply acting strong, keeping a "stiff upper lip," and wading through it like a martyr. It involves feeling the pain, wearing the grief, and still knowing God is faithful.

So how do you stand on the banks of a wide river of pain, bitterness, and even shame and be able to see what is waiting on the other side of the bridge? Well, you don't. There is no way to see what redemption lies on the other side of your pain. Your leap of faith is in trusting that every tragic moment in your life has a ripple effect, and that blessings and hardships are the brick and mortar of the bridge that gets you to the other side of your misery.

Stowe had begun the process of healing her self-destructing body when she encountered Jean Bertram, but she needed to grieve on the misery side of her past before she could experience the full redemption and definition of healing—namely through *forgiveness*.

CHAPTER FIFTEEN

SEEDS OF FORGIVENESS

"Judge not, and you will not be judged;
condemn not, and you will not be condemned;
forgive, and you will be forgiven."

—LUKE 6:37 ESV

Stowe's Journey

The months following Dad's death were, of course, difficult as I faced the anguish of missing the man I had sometimes hated—but also always loved. I missed our telephone conversations most of all. Over the last few years we had talked on the phone at least once a day.

Dealing with funeral arrangements, wills, and legalities were a hassle, but perhaps the most difficult thing for me was handling all the guilt I felt about our last few days together. I was haunted by not only my father's selfishness, but also my own. *How could we have let ourselves treat each other that way?*

The shame and remorse I felt over my own immaturity was so great I could hardly go on at times. I often wondered if I was madder at my father or myself. I had to do something to get past these feelings. *But what?*

I knew in my heart that God extends the gift of forgiveness to us all; so I prayed about forgiving my father. *Yes*, I decided, *I could forgive him . . . But could I forgive myself?* I decided to start with him. I began just saying the words—*I forgive you, Dad*—to myself. Sometimes I would even say them out loud. At first it felt as if I were saying a lie, but the more I repeated it, the more I began to genuinely feel it in my heart. And once I got to the point where I could actually *feel* sympathy and forgiveness for this man (a regular human being like myself), I found I could also *feel* compassion and forgiveness for myself. What a blessed relief.

Of course, this didn't happen overnight. It has been a long walk to my healing—one that has involved tears, times of solitude, prayer, and forgiveness. And in the end, it could not have happened without the willing ears of a few close friends and family.

Talking has been one of the most cathartic keys to my healing process. After many conversations with Peter and a few very close friends, I understood that Dad's poor choices during my childhood were not because he didn't love me; they were a direct result of a deep denial of his own pain and the alcoholism that was the fruition of that pain. As a young man my father suffered from a poor self-image and began drinking at an early age to cover up his shyness. In those days, drinking was a socially acceptable way of dealing with every life situation—in fact, it was so accepted that his mother had actually given him a monogrammed silver hip flask as a graduation gift!

Drinking was a way of life for both my parents, and after my mother's death, Dad continued to use alcohol as a crutch to carry him through his unbearable grief. Relying on alcohol to drown his sorrows was the catalyst of many poor choices my father made as a parent. Yes, I know alcohol is no excuse for a person's bad parental judgment, but at least I was finally beginning to understand the reasons *why* he made the choices he made.

I learned something horrific about my father shortly before he died. He told me that when my mother was dying of cancer and he was at his lowest point of despair, he actually thought about killing all of us. Imagine a man with so much grief and agony that he can't bear to live without his wife, but he can't bear to die without his children. He had felt trapped with no way to escape.

And when at last I understood that he was just a flawed person (like myself) and not some superhuman hero, it was easier to forgive him. Here is the bottom line: I forgive Dad because, ultimately, I know he was not an evil person. I love him because I finally know he did the best he could with what he had—as we all do. Dad was under the influence of something that promotes an evil ripple effect of disconnection in the world. Because of his pain and alcoholism, he couldn't be counted on to act in his *own* best interest; so, realistically speaking, how could he be counted on to act in mine? I understand now that his alcoholism stunted his growth, prevented him from facing the pains that may have otherwise matured into wisdom. If Dad hadn't medicated his pain, he may have eventually seen how our lives are all linked and we have great responsibilities to one another.

If the cycle of pain had perpetuated itself, I wouldn't be writing this. I would be immobilized by my resentment, chained up with anger, weighed down by bitterness. And I'd be passing that poison on to my daughters through the slow, intravenous drip of a life less lived. But, fortunately,

I learned to share my feelings of pain rather than hold them inside—as I had done so many times in the past—and I was freed to move on with my life.

Writing this has helped me so much. Once pain is verbalized, or written down, it can no longer lurk in the shadows of denial—it loses its teeth. By facing my fears and my past and forgiving my father, I can now stand in the light of truth. In doing so I have been free to pray for and accept healing for myself.

✦

Peter
Is there a link between physical or emotional wellness and the capacity to forgive? In Mark 2:4–12, Jesus makes clear the connection between forgiveness of sin and prayers for healing:

Since they could not get him to Jesus because of the crowd, they made an opening in the roof above Jesus and, after digging through it, lowered the mat the paralyzed man was lying on. When Jesus saw their faith, he said to the paralytic, "Son, your sins are forgiven." Now some teachers of the law were sitting there, thinking to themselves, "Why does this fellow talk like that? He's blaspheming! Who can forgive sins but God alone?" Immediately Jesus knew in his spirit that this was what they were thinking in their hearts, and he said to them, "Why are you thinking these things? Which is easier to say to the paralytic, 'Your sins are forgiven,' or to say, 'Get up, take your mat and walk'? But that you may know that the Son of Man has authority on earth to forgive sins. . . ." He said to the paralytic, "I tell you, get up, take your mat and go home." He got up, took his mat and walked out in full view of them all. (N I V)

Later in Mark's Gospel, Jesus extends the power of forgiveness to His followers. And not only does He connect it to their ability to pray, He links it back to their own need to accept God's forgiveness for themselves:

> And when you stand praying, if you hold anything against anyone, forgive him, so that you Father in heaven may forgive you your sins. (M A R K   1 1 : 2 5   N K J V)

Praying for God's forgiveness triggers a chain of circumstances, which allows for the miraculous healing of broken spiritual connections. First, it requires us to acknowledge our own responsibility as decision-makers in the overall scheme of life. That doesn't mean we necessarily have a choice in suffering as it occurs; but it does recognize the fact that we are personally responsible for how we *respond* to our suffering. Second, it requires us to confess that we are just as guilty of being disconnected and self-absorbed as the people we hate. Third, it forces us to admit that we are powerless without God's help. And finally, an important *dual connection* is healed by accepting God's forgiveness as we forgive those who have sinned against us. Without accepting God's forgiveness for ourselves, we remain forever cut off from His miraculous healing power.

There is only one power source that is able to transform a heart so broken into one so full of hope. Stowe and I have both encountered this power in our lives, and it has completely transformed us.

THE COMMANDMENT TO LOVE

*You shall not bow down to them or serve them, for
I the LORD your God am a jealous God, visiting the
iniquity of the fathers on the children to the third
and the fourth generation of those who hate me,
but showing steadfast love to thousands of those
who love me and keep my commandments.*
—SECOND COMMANDMENT, EXOD. 20:5–6 ESV

The Second Commandment, especially the Old Covenant ideas
of disobedience and punishment, take a while to unpack in
light of the New Covenant promise of God's loving forgiveness (Jer. 31:33–34; Ezek. 36:25–28), but there are two things
that catch my interest most. First, I am impressed by the
love/hate ratio, which shows *love* to be geometrically more
powerful—not to mention more rewarding—than *hate*. And
second, I see how the consequences for our actions are passed
along to future generations. Sometimes the inherited "sin of
the fathers" cannot be explained entirely by genetics as *original sin*. Evil ideas are often passed along to us by the teachings
and examples of our family or culture.

FORGIVENESS AND RACIAL HATRED

Racial and religious hatreds are perhaps the most deadly deceptions, not only for our own souls, but also for the peace of
the world. And when religious doctrine promotes racial hatred
and unforgiveness, it creates in us a double disconnection,

with people . . . and with God. Piety combined with prejudice automatically breaks the greatest of commandments:

> Love the Lord your God with all your heart and with all your soul and with all your mind. . . . Love your neighbor as yourself. (MATT. 22:37, 39 NIV)

How can we possibly hold onto racial prejudice and unforgiveness if our spirit is enlightened by God's love? Louis Farrakhan has been one of our generation's most inflammatory spokesmen for the African-American organization, Nation of Islam. His antiwhite and anti-Semitic statements have gained worldwide attention, and he has been accused of inciting racial fury for many years. However, on December 23, 1999, the *Washington Post* published a surprising news story of an event that had taken place the previous day:

RECOVERING FARRAKHAN URGES UNITY, FORGIVENESS[*]

Making his first public appearance in nearly a year, Nation of Islam leader Louis Farrakhan today said a "near-death experience" with prostate cancer had left him a changed man as he preached a message of forgiveness and unity among all races and religions.

Standing with Catholic priests, Jewish rabbis, and Muslim clerics at a news conference at the Nation of Islam mosque in Chicago's South Side, Farrakhan looked fit and his voice was strong as he spoke in conciliatory tones about the need for all religions to come together on Christmas Day and "pray, not for a change in someone else, but for a change in ourselves."[1]

[*] © 1999, *The Washington Post*. Reprinted with permission.

Farrakhan arrived at death's doorstep following complications from radiation-related ulcers that had not fully healed. In this speech that shocked the world, his dramatic turnabout from radical racism was palpable. He went on to say:

"Only through our act of atonement can we be forgiven for what we have said or done to injure other human beings— a member of another race or a member of another religious group, another nation or another ethnic group."[2]

What else but a face-to-face encounter with God could motivate such a turnaround in a person? The *Washington Post* article gave further clues to the extent of Farrakhan's newfound insights, which took on a prophetic tone:

Despite his illness, Farrakhan displayed some of his trademark passion and fiery rhetoric as, his voice rising, he warned of apocalyptic prophecies in the Bible, the Torah and the Koran and warned that "dark clouds of a great war are now rising" throughout the world.

"Famine, pestilence, earthquakes and 'a time of trouble as never seen before' could usher in the new millennium if people of all religions fail to come together to embrace God," Farrakhan warned.[3]

To give witness to the depth of Louis Farrakhan's profound transformation, listen to the remarks he made about the very core of a religion that he had previously scorned:

"We are asking that this Christmas not be observed with drunkenness, frivolity, filth and foolishness, mocking the name of Jesus the Christ," he said. "Instead of making it (Christmas) a holiday, we are asking to make it a holy day."

The Nation of Islam leader reserved his most stinging rebuke for one of the most commonplace symbols of Christmas: Santa Claus.

"We here and others are asking that Santa Claus be put in his proper place. Santa Claus is a falsehood. Jesus Christ is the truth," Farrakhan said.[4]

I would have been naturally suspicious of such a passionate speech from an extremist as prolific as Farrakhan had I not studied so many other stories of lives and attitudes changed following near-death experiences and a direct encounter with the Light of God. But I can appreciate the extraordinary bridge that a die-hard racist has crossed, when he now urges people of *all colors and religions* to "pray, not for a change in someone else, but for a change in ourselves."

> *When you put a seed into the ground, it doesn't*
> *grow into a plant unless it dies first. And what you*
> *put in the ground is not the plant that will grow,*
> *but only a dry little seed of wheat or whatever it is*
> *you are planting. Then God gives it a new body—*
> *just the kind he wants it to have.*
>
> —1 COR. 15:36–38 NLT

CHAPTER SIXTEEN

THE HEALING BEGINS

> *My dear friends, we must not live to satisfy our*
> *desires. If you do, you will die. But you will live, if*
> *by the help of God's Spirit you say "No" to your*
> *desires. Only those people who are led by God's*
> *Spirit are his children. God's Spirit doesn't make us*
> *slaves who are afraid of him. Instead, we become*
> *his children and call him our Father. God's Spirit*
> *makes us sure that we are his children. His Spirit*
> *lets us know that together with Christ we will*
> *be given what God has promised. We will also*
> *share in the glory of Christ, because we have*
> *suffered with him.*
>
> —ROM. 8:12–17 CEV

Stowe's Journey

In the last six years since my father's death, I have continued to feel great changes in my spirit—an awakening to a part of me I have never acknowledged. After finally admitting that I hurt, that I was a child of abuse, I am finally able to *feel* happiness. I thank God for helping me become aware of the inner voices that worked to hold me back for much of my life.

Until a few years ago I never really *heard* the steady stream of discouraging words that flowed through my mind, but I did *listen* to them. Those words were a constant reminder to me that my legs are too skinny, that I am not as bright as so and so, that I am not good at math, and that I have never really been successful—and probably never will be.

Now I have to wonder, *Why in the world would I or anyone else ever listen to such ugly words of discouragement?* I know why: Because we are not aware of them; or perhaps we are aware of their existence, but we have grown comfortable with them—we accept them as truth.

From the time we are born, we are programmed by our parents, our siblings, our friends, and our successes and failures, all of which are giving us messages—some good, some not so good, and some downright self-defeating. And as we listen to them over and over in our minds, they are shaping who we are and who we will be, either helping us accomplish our life's mission or keeping us from it.

The tapes are rolling. Stop and listen. What are they saying?

I've often wondered why some people seem to be able to succeed in whatever they try, despite difficult setbacks. I have watched as they dig themselves out of complete financial ruin, unbearable family difficulties, and a host of other trials and tribulations. So how do they do it?

Is their faith greater than mine?

Are they praying the "right" way?

Are they more deserving than I?

It's easy to go into a negative frame of mind when it seems that all *your* prayers aren't being answered and you're living a life of "not enough" and all you want is a life of "just enough"; especially when it seems plenty of other people you know are blessed with a life of "more than enough." But it's not about praying the "right" way, or saying the right words to God. God isn't a dancing dog at a circus; He doesn't do parlor tricks on command for our benefit or amusement. We can't *bribe* Him with anything to make Him do our bidding. And no one deserves blessings any more than the next person. We're all sinners. Psalms 103:10 says, "*He has not punished us as our sins should be punished; He has not repaid us for the evil we have done*" (NKJV).

If you do believe it's all about posture and protocol, how do you explain the many people who *do not believe* God is in control of their lives, and yet they still accomplish great things and gather unbelievable wealth and power? It's hard to reconcile that with the millions of people who pray for help yet remain powerless and tossed around in life's forbidding ocean.

I can't imagine any life lived without faith in God, particularly my own life—no matter how circuitously painful my circumstances are at any given moment. But I've discovered what most winning personalities (believers *and* nonbelievers) already know: The answer to a successful life lies in our sheer will, which propels us to march forward. Our spirit of perseverance fuels our determination to survive and to create. One of the most precious gifts God gives us is our spirit, which He breathed into us in the beginning, and includes His character traits of creating things through both word and will. So I can't help but find it a bit ironic that unbelievers, even in the mover-and-shaker variety, seem unaware that they are made in God's image. I know their real power comes from the true power source.

Successful people also share a common message refrain: *IT CAN BE DONE!*

"I tell you the truth, if you have faith as small as a mustard seed, you can say to this mountain, 'Move from here to there' and it will move. Nothing will be impossible for you." (M A T T . 1 7 : 2 0 NIV)

People who thrive in life know, either through instinct or training, that there is great power in words—both the words inside their subconscious and the spoken word. Words are what we all use to create something from nothing, or to change one thing into something else. In the story of Genesis, God created the universe with *words*. Look around you—see what you've created for yourself? You are already living the life you've imagined, and you are constantly reinforcing it with your words.

The surprising thing to many people is that this dynamic, creative principle works two ways: You can create either positive or negative blueprints for the life you are building, by what you habitually say about yourself. And due to the creative power of your words, your life will attract and manifest the realities contained within your most dominant thoughts. This is worth repeating: *Because of the creative power of your words, your life will attract and manifest the realities contained within your most dominant thoughts.* Your words become real—that's what spoken prayer is about. *"Therefore I tell you, whatever you ask in prayer, believe that you have received it, and it will be yours"* (Mark 1 1 : 2 4 ESV).

Discerning Your Inner Voices

Here's a little quiz to see which direction you are taking in life—positive or negative—based on the words you choose.

1. I'm making a _____ with my life.
2. I always _____ at parties.
3. When it comes to money, I am _____.
4. It seems like everyone I meet thinks I am _____.
5. My purpose in life seems to be _____.
6. The choices I make in life are typically _____.

Psychologists use the word *subconscious* to describe our inner voices—the ones that roll like a tape player in our minds. For some, the voices are warm, friendly, and sprinkled with encouragement. For others, the messages undercut their confidence, wound their heart, and impede their progress on a daily basis. I lived in this latter state most of my life, so I had to learn to take action and consciously exert my will over these negative voices. Then I had to learn how to re-record the message.

The subconscious must be brought into the conscious. I did this by making a verbal agreement with myself that I would make a change for the better. I vowed to listen for my voices when I was frustrated, angry, or sad. Then I promised to rebuke the negative voices and even replace them with something positive. It wasn't easy. When I am in a high state of aggravation or frustration, it's hard to change the course of my runaway train. But even with a full head of steam, *it can be done!*

It really doesn't take long to start seeing results—if you keep your mind focused on your goal. And if you slip up a little, be gentle and forgive yourself. It's not the end of the world; just consider it a learning experience.

Here are a few of the negatively programmed messages I allowed myself to hear over the years. Some of them may sound familiar.

"*Oh, I am such an idiot! I ruined the whole project.*"

"*I could never be good at business. I'm so disorganized. Besides I don't have any business skills.*"

"*I'm just like my father/mother. I'll never amount to anything.*"

"*Oh, no, not again! I always do that!*"

"*I'll never be able to control my temper, and I'm afraid I'm going to hurt somebody someday.*"

I began reprogramming my negative voices with the goal of learning to be gentle with myself. I made an effort to talk to myself as I would a small child. As is the case with children, harsh tones and language and name-calling are particularly detrimental. The next time you hear your own negatively programmed messages, try this technique. And remember that you are trying to encourage yourself. Replace those old voices with some new ones:

Negative voice: "*Oh, I am such an idiot! I ruined the whole project.*"

Positive new voice: "*I made a mistake. But I've learned a valuable lesson from it, and I will try to not make that mistake again.*"

Negative voice: "*I could never be any good at business. I'm so disorganized. Besides I don't have any business skills.*"

Positive new voice: "*I bet I could get someone to help show me how to get organized, and if I really studied and worked at it I could do it!*"

Negative voice: "*I'm just like my father/mother. I'll never amount to anything.*"

Positive new voice: "*I am my own person and I have unique abilities. I am doing something worthwhile with my life.*"

Negative voice: "*Oh, no, not again! I always do that!*"
Positive new voice: "*No, I do not always do that—this is only the second time it has happened. And I am going to work at it until it doesn't happen again.*"

Negative voice: "*I'll never be able to control my temper, and I'm afraid I'm going to hurt somebody someday.*"
New voice: "*I realize I have a temper, but I am working hard to find the source of my anger and a way to diffuse it. It is within my power, by God's grace, to live peacefully.*"

It feels so good to say that, with God's help and a lot of effort on my part, I am winning the war against my negative programs. I've learned to recognize the negative messages—I know their tone, and I know how they rob me of my happiness. They are simply lies that were fed to me as a child. But I am old enough now to find my own voice and take charge of the words that create my life.

✣

Peter
Crossing the bridge to healing and a life of connectedness is a choice every person can make. Lee McRee is a man who made that choice, rejecting the racist chants that echoed in his mind since his childhood. For him it began with a seemingly impassable chasm: racism versus his own deeply rooted belief system.

LEE McREE'S ENLIGHTENMENT

Lee McRee is a white man raised in the Deep South. On one sweltering summer night in the late 1950s, he was the first police officer to respond to a fire alarm, which brought him directly into the all-black neighborhood on the east side of Mount Dora, Florida. As he stood outside the burning house, his was the only white face among the growing crowd of worried onlookers.

A young woman in her bathrobe pulled hysterically on Lee's arm, shrieking, "My baby! Where's my baby? Who's got my baby?" The child's father was just as frantic, and both parents were too terrified to go back into their home, which was quickly being consumed by the flames.

Lee hesitated, weighing the choice before him. In that moment, his entire life's training—as a southern, white, churchgoing police officer, together with all the baggage of bigotry and conflicting value judgments concerning the life of a little black baby—came fully into account.

It wasn't the first time he had to make a choice between what he had been taught and what he felt compelled to do.

Lee was born and raised in Mount Dora in the pre–World War II era of the Deep South. He was schooled to believe that blacks were genetically inferior to whites. He had been indoctrinated by a peculiar religious teaching known as the "curse of Ham," which was one of the cornerstones of white supremacy reasoning. This dogma proposed that Noah had cursed his son Ham, whose people would become a slave race in service to his brothers Shem's and Japheth's descendants. That scripture became linked with the notion that Ham's lineage migrated to Africa, while the other brothers traveled northward to Europe. Therefore, according to this thin patchwork of reasoning, it was not only acceptable but biblically dictated that black people should be the slaves, servants, or at least subordinates of whites.

To understand how deeply rooted this thinking goes, consider this old essay that explains the curse of Ham to Aryan students in nineteenth-century Mississippi:

> The wayward son had contaminated his own race by marrying into the race of Cain, who, in consequence of having slain his brother Abel, had been smitten with a black skin. On this account, all of Ham's descendants, and not merely those of Canaan, were Africans or Negroes. On the other hand, Shem and Japheth were blessed with white descendants because they had married within their own race. It was only right therefore that the degenerate black descendants of Ham were doomed to perpetual servitude to the superior white offspring of Shem and Japheth.[1]

This was the kind of religious, fundamentalist propaganda that was accepted by the culture of Lee's childhood. And Lee's family also taught him to hate blacks; so for Lee, hatred was a fact of life. But at the age of twelve, Lee had a deeply moving spiritual experience. He became "saved," and that began a long journey of trying to separate truth from lies. Although he still held fast to his racist attitudes, he began to realize that God was working on his heart.

When Lee joined the air force in 1954, he went to basic training in upper New York State and faced a racial culture shock. In the first days of camp, Lee was confronted by a knife-wielding black recruit from Brooklyn who had been taught to hate whites as much as Lee had been taught to hate "n—s." Fortunately, the fight was diffused and both were reprimanded. But as fate would have it, Lee and his antagonist were assigned to share a tent, which forced the two to talk about their lives and upbringings. It didn't take long to realize that if they went to war, they would be protecting each other's backs, so their hatred, as Lee saw it, was "toned down to a mutual dislike."

Later, when Lee was appointed to a base in Texas, he was again paired with a black roommate. The two men became best friends, and their friendship lasted for many years. By then, Lee was beginning to see God's hand in trying to reshape his heart and mind regarding race and religion.

Upon Lee's next transfer, he knew for sure the Lord was arranging his education in racial tolerance. At his new base in Bermuda, which was 80 percent black, Lee found himself attending a black church. He became the choir director . . . of an all-black choir. After a painful kidney stone surgery, he was relocated yet again—this time to Montgomery, Alabama. A black therapist, whom Lee greatly appreciated and respected for his skill and positive attitude, assisted his rehabilitation.

Despite everything that had happened to him, Lee McRee still clung to a tiny piece of pride that he was part of a superior race, so his heart struggled with the compassion that had grown for so many black people. Lee said, "God was smoothing out my rough edges to prepare me for the inevitability of what was about to happen."

THE BRIDGE TO BLOODY SUNDAY

The year was 1965, and the civil rights movement had begun gathering momentum. Black voters still didn't have equal rights in Alabama or Mississippi, and Gov. George Wallace of Alabama was determined that would never happen.

Lee McRee was part of a southern gospel quartet that accompanied Governor Wallace's campaign tour. Lee had also joined up with the Montgomery County Constables, the mounted police for that town.

On March 7, the Reverend Martin Luther King Jr. was supposed to help lead a march from Selma to Montgomery, the capital of Alabama, to protest the state's use of violence against civil rights workers. But George Wallace refused to allow the march to take place. King went immediately to Washington, D.C., and petitioned President Lyndon Johnson for federal authorization to march. It looked like the rally would have to be postponed until the next day—Monday, March 8. But the people of Selma decided not to wait, and they began the march toward Montgomery without Reverend King.

As the marchers arrived at the Edmund Pettus Bridge in Montgomery, a posse of two hundred state troopers met them. Among the constables on horseback was Lee McRee. He and the others were armed with clubs fashioned from oak branches. Lee had been trained to use his horse's neck to gently push back crowds, and he understood that he and the other constables would be using that technique to keep the marchers from crossing the bridge.

He was positioned behind the second row of officers when he saw something that shook him to his soul. As the black marchers stopped on the bridge, unable to proceed further, they bowed their heads and began to pray to God. Without warning, the police officers in the front row raised their clubs and began beating the heads of those in the midst of their prayers. The scene turned chaotic, and although Lee never raised his club, he saw things he would never forget . . . marchers beaten, men being thrown from the bridge into the icy river, and blood . . . lots of blood.

The officers succeeded in beating the crowds back into the housing projects of Selma. There, even the residents who hadn't been involved in the march were beaten. The first day of the march went down in history books as Bloody Sunday.

With the bridge not yet crossed, the Reverends Martin Luther King Jr. and Ralph Abernathy were present on Tuesday, March 9. Their passionate preaching stirred the spirit of the crowds, who were now determined to cross the bridge—no matter how many were beaten, no matter how many were killed. They were going to march on to Montgomery.

Already disturbed by what he had witnessed on the first day of the march, Lee McRee once again mounted his horse and proceeded toward the Edmund Pettus Bridge. When he was within three hundred feet of King and Abernathy, who were flanked by hundreds of other black marchers, McRee stopped dead in his tracks. In the middle of what would soon become a pivot point in the story of human liberty, Lee heard a booming voice speak to him. *"This is wrong! What are you doing here?"*

Lee instinctively turned to find the origin of the voice, but there were only constables, and none had spoken to him. He then recognized what he had heard . . . the commanding voice had come from within him . . . and God was speaking to his heart!

Lee paused for a moment, and then he backed off with his horse, going directly to his captain. He explained how he felt it wasn't right to be there and requested to be dismissed. He was given permission to load up his horse and Lee left the scene.

That second day of the march turned out to be even worse than the first—more bloodshed, beatings, and hundreds of arrests. A white minister, who had been a march supporter, was beaten to death, as was a woman supporter from Detroit. The news was now big enough to warrant federal action, and on the third day of the march, National Guard troops were sent to escort the marchers to the capitol in Montgomery. This became a major defeat for Governor Wallace and the States' Rights group, which opposed the blacks. It was a turning point in the battle for civil rights.

For Lee McRee, it was an important moment in his understanding that God does not favor, or curse, anyone for the color of his or her skin. He turned in his badge and his gun, resigning not only from his constable position, but also from the States' Rights Party. He had personally witnessed a historic drama in which humanity's freedom to choose between man's way and the Lord's way won a major victory in favor of God. And Lee feels that his own choice, which he made that day, was a critical step in connecting closer to God's Spirit.

But many years after that momentous event, Lee had another choice to make, and he didn't have the benefit of a booming voice from heaven. With no more than a moment's thought, Officer McRee broke down the door of that burning Mount Dora house.

Lee dropped to the ground and entered a bedroom. Smoke filled his lungs and nearly blinded his eyes. He couldn't see anything in the small bed, but he could hear a tiny cry coming from somewhere in the acrid smoke. *"Where are you?"* he called out. Then he saw the slight movement of a white blanket heaped on the floor. The cries were coming from under the heap! In a flash Lee scooped up the little bundle and dashed out the door.

A split second later the roof came crashing down into the blazing house. The hysterical mother grabbed her little boy, and with tears streaming down her face she fell to her knees and thanked God.

Against Lee's protests, the local paper splashed the story across the headlines: LOCAL HERO: POLICEMAN SAVES CHILD.

I asked Lee, many years later, whether things might have been different if not for his previous experience at the bridge in Selma. "Absolutely," Lee said, shaking his head. "If God had not spoken to me that day of the march—and been at work changing my heart so completely over the years—the *old* Lee would probably have just stood there and watched that house burn down." And then, with a faraway look, he confessed, "In fact, at an earlier time, I probably would have wanted to push the parents back in it. But, by that point in my life, God had so changed my heart and my mind that I knew His message to me was, '*Lee . . . that's a LIFE in there! I created that life. Your job is to protect that life. Now, GO GET IT!*' "[2]

At the time I interviewed him, Lee was a strong and solidly built man, even in his mid-sixties. But it wasn't unusual to see him choking back tears when he talked about the journey God had taken him on. "I don't always know where He's leading . . . but I'm doing my best to follow." Those who know Lee would attest to his sensitivity to people and say he has a way of knowing when others are in need of help or friendship.

Today, McRee says if had the chance to go back in time and tell twelve-year-old Lee the truth about racism, he would whisper in his ear, "This is wrong. . . . Listen to your heart. . . . We've got to love one another, just like you want to be loved!"

> *This is My commandment, that you love one an-*
> *other as I have loved you. Greater love has no one*
> *than this, than to lay down one's life for his friends.*
>
> —JOHN 15:12–13 NKJV

CHAPTER SEVENTEEN

RECONNECTING: BODY, MIND, AND SPIRIT

*Now the end of all things is near; therefore, be
clear-headed and disciplined for prayer. Above all,
keep your love for one another at full strength, since
love covers a multitude of sins.*

—1 PETER 4:7–8 HCSB

Stowe's Journey

So maybe we are all walking wounded. What should we do about it? Dredge up those old memories? Sit down and cry? Talk about them? Write about them? Seek professional counseling? Pray to God for help? The answer, of course, is "Yes!" to all of the above. It's not an easy process, but having the weight of the world lifted from my shoulders was well worth the effort and any discomfort associated with it.

If you're reading this now and you feel a tugging in your heart, if you know somewhere deep inside your spirit there are wounds that never healed, consider this your *call to arms*. It's time to do battle with those haunting voices from the past, time to heal the hurt of that little girl or little boy within you.

The good news is that you don't have to do it alone.

God is doing miracles every day in this department; all it takes is summoning the courage to admit that *you have pain* and then asking for help.

Go ahead and say it out loud: *I am an abused child*—or whatever it was that wounded your tender heart. Admit your own pain.

After saying it, be ready to feel sad. You're a small child with a big hurt that needs a tender kiss before your healing can begin. The most painful part of healing from a cut or a broken bone is the fixing and reconnecting of nerves around the wound. Your healing is nothing less than the reconnection of your broken soul, by the eternally loving Spirit of God within you.

You may have already prayed for your healing, and maybe it seems nothing has changed. Please don't lose hope. I encourage you to pray for inspiration on how your healing will begin. Perhaps it will include seeking out a wise counselor; maybe you'll start forgiving those who have hurt you—you may even begin to forgive yourself; perhaps you'll find help for addictions; and maybe you'll seek out and keep company with those who will give you their love and support at this critical time in your life.

If you're not ready to take these steps right now, perhaps it's not time. But know that there will come a day when your soul will long to break free from the shackles of your past, and you'll look squarely in the eyes of your fear, pain, and frustration. It won't be a painless process, but just imagine how free you will be to move forward in your life.

I am personally feeling a new surge of energy in my soul since I came to terms with the ghost from my past. It's given me a kind of confidence I had never known, an ability to push further beyond my fears. My accomplishments, no matter how small, encourage me. The negative voices of long ago continue to be replaced by loving words and phrases that lift me up in times of need. I know my education as a human being is nowhere near complete. In fact, I believe it may have just begun. But it's a wonderful journey and I thank God for it every day.

So I encourage those of you who are hurting. I urge you to at least consider what life could be like without the pain and the invisible bonds of your past. Think about it. Imagine, and clearly visualize yourself with a different outlook.

How would it feel to be truly happy?

What would your life be like without the boundaries of anger and resentment?

What would you do without bitterness and pain?

How would your dreams look if you didn't live in fear?

How far could you go if you truly knew the depth of God's love for you?

I believe your newfound happiness and unchained dreams could make you and this planet a better place. In fact, I am sure of it; for by healing the wounds within ourselves, we take the first step in healing the wounds of this world and reconnecting the spirit within us all.

Some readers may be thinking, *Gee, she certainly doesn't seem to have any problem going on and on with her story and her revelations of life.* Be assured that, years ago, I would have been paralyzed at the thought of writing my life story. I could not even admit to *myself* what I had been through, much less share—or rather *burden*—other people with the details. Besides, I was in the habit of constantly comparing myself with other people, so it was easier to just deny my own pain—I reasoned that others had suffered much worse injustice than I had. And the little problems of my life could not possibly compare with those of, say, Holocaust survivors or starving children of Third World countries.

Maybe, if there *was* such a thing as an atrocities chart, my problems would not compare with those of others, but I'm not talking about comparison charts—I am finally admitting that, during my personal journey of life, I have acquired a few wounds. That's all. We all have.

Somewhere deep down inside of every person there are wounds that are tender and often too painful to recall. Like monster movies from our childhood, they haunt us—a parent whose criticism was unceasing; a sibling who was a constant tormentor; a best friend who, with just a few words, broke our heart; parents who abandoned us for no reason or were emotionally unavailable; teachers or authority figures who made us feel inferior or out of place; and people who—with or without knowing it— somehow drained the love for life out of us when we were too young to even know what life is supposed to be.

Does any of this sound familiar? You may be tempted to say, "Well, that was a long time ago—it really doesn't bother me now." And maybe it doesn't bother you *on the surface,* but often these unhealed wounds of our childhood bleed over into our adult lives and affect the way we function in this world and how we deal with others.

Though many people spend their lives denying anything is wrong with them, they are usually aware on some level that they *are* hurting. Unexplained depression, outbursts of anger, an inability to accomplish goals, and a feeling of general unhappiness about themselves and life are just some of the symptoms that plague people who are on the run from the truth.

There are many ways to deaden the pain—some people take pills or pour alcohol on their wounds, some criticize or bully those around them in an attempt to hide their own insecurities. Some people simply close up and say nothing, and still others try to squelch the hurtful voices within by burying themselves in work, sex, sports, their children, or any one of a million things. But as any good doctor will admit—*killing the pain does not treat the disease.* And until you realize and admit that there is suffering—suffering in your own soul as well as in the world—you cannot pray for healing.

> *For this reason I remind you to fan into flame the gift of*
> *God, which is in you through the laying on of my*
> *hands. For God did not give us a spirit of timidity, but*
> *a spirit of power, of love and of self-discipline.*
>
> —2 TIM. 1 : 6 – 7 NIV

Peter

As you've seen, Stowe has followed her heart into some wonderful new domains, which have yielded great blessings for her and for our family. By working through the tragedy of her father's death by cancer—the disease that has taken most of her family members—and then struggling to be free of the devastating weight of her past, Stowe has become well educated in many areas of growth and healing. One particular area that Stowe has become somewhat of an expert on is *preventive* health maintenance. This may have led us into some positive lifestyle changes as a family, but it literally saved her life.

Stowe

This is not a book about health and nutrition, so I won't go into *too* much detail concerning my studies of it over the last few years; however, it should be noted that there is a definite connection between body, mind, and spirit—one that I believe cannot be ignored.

I don't consider eating Twinkies, hamburgers, sodas, and other fast foods sinful—and they will never keep God from loving us; but I do think our society's dependence upon these products may cause our bodies to be unwell. Too much energy spent on digesting heavy food can also dull our senses and take the edge off our mental abilities to connect with ourselves as well as others.

And since this *is* a book about healing, I have to say that I believe the Creator designed our bodies to be *self-healing*. In fact, what we call *miraculous healing* might actually be considered an acceleration of what our bodies are designed to do naturally.

It is wonderful to think that God can make us well through miraculous intervention using the hands of His servants to transmit His healing energy. But what is equally exciting is that by using God's original plan of eating healthful, natural, and living foods, our bodies are designed to make themselves well! Here is just one more area of my life that could have had a tragic outcome, but once again, God stepped in and provided the light I needed to find my way.

CANCER COMES HOME

Cancer took two of my grandparents and both my parents as well as my foster brother, Joey. Three of my cousins have also battled various types of cancer. Looking around, one can't help but notice how many people in this world are suffering from this killer disease. I remember back in 2002, when I first became aware that almost every week someone in our little country church was standing up to ask for prayer for a friend or loved one who had cancer. I admit I became a little obsessed about the subject.

It became clear to me at that time that if I didn't do anything and everything possible for prevention, it would not just be a matter of *if* I would get cancer but, rather, *when*. And with these dismal thoughts, I also found myself wondering, *What course of action would I take if I did get cancer?* I knew the medical world has had some success with chemotherapy and radiation to combat the disease, but judging by the results I've seen—the weakened body, the sickness, the temporary turn for the better, and then having the cancer return again, usually for the last and fatal conclusion—I was convinced I never wanted to go that route. Still, I wondered, *What would I do?*

Jean Bertram must have continued praying for me long after our time together, because several weeks after she helped bring healing to my terrible rash, I made a memorable trip to the library that ended up changing my life. In those days, when our girls were much younger, a visit to the library usually meant getting a stack of books just for them. I simply had no time to read. But that day, for some reason, I felt inspired to get something for myself. I was immediately drawn to two books; one looked like light reading and was on the general health of women; the other was a more challenging, academic book dealing with cancer and how diet contributes to this devastating disease.

I brought my books home, eager to settle back into my easy

chair and start reading. I had just begun when the phone interrupted my peace. It was the nurse from my doctor's office:

"Mrs. Shockey . . ." came a serious-sounding voice. "This is Cyndee from Dr. Johnson's office. I'm afraid I've got some bad news from your pap smear results. You have precancerous cells in your cervix—which is pretty serious. Now, it doesn't mean you have cancer, but these cells could cause cancer in that area. We'll have to do a procedure, which basically burns out the precancerous cells. I'll need to schedule an appointment with a specialist to see you as soon as possible."

I hung up the phone, feeling a sudden knot in my stomach, and sank back into my chair. My mind reeled with the news. *Precancerous cells—in my body! God, what next?* My heart raced. Then, like a weird scene from *The Twilight Zone,* my attention gravitated back to my new library books about *cancer* and *women's health.* I had picked out these books . . . at this particular time . . . when I had absolutely no clue that my pap tests would come back anything less than normal. Yet I have come to recognize God's hand in times like these, and I quickly realized He had guided me to pick out those books, just before I really needed them. *Was there something in these books I needed to know—some bit of information that might help me?* I began to pore over them.

No sooner had I started reading than I was interrupted once more, this time by the doorbell. It turned out to be a good friend of ours, Jack Rogers, who would be an overnight guest as he passed through town. It had been several months since we had seen Jack, so we sat and chatted, catching up on the latest news.

Then, flashing a big smile, Jack reached into his bag and pulled out a book. "Stowe," he said, excitedly. "I've just discovered something that is radically changing my life. I thought you might be interested in it." I read the title: *God's Way to Ultimate Health* by Dr. George Malkmus. As I flipped through the pages, Jack gave me a summary of what he had learned about the dangers of eating certain foods. He explained that optimum health could be obtained from making a concerted lifestyle change; eating what Dr. Malkmus calls "living foods" rather than cooked foods, which are mostly devoid of living enzymes and vitamins. What Malkmus advises eating is a diet rich in fruits, nuts, seeds, and uncooked vegetables. He also claims that, through this biblically based diet, literally thousands of people have been healed of everything from cancer to heart disease, funguses to arthritis, and, in short, just about anything that ails the human body.

I leaned back in my chair and listened intently to Jack's words, my eyes wide with wonder. My mouth wasn't exactly watering at the thought of eating raw food, but I was definitely getting the feeling that *God was trying to tell me something important!* In fact, it felt like I was being hit over the head. *Okay, God! Okay! I'm listening!* I thought to myself. *I'll read these books. Just give me some time.*

The next day we were scheduled to take a weekend trip. Jack said I could borrow the book for a few days until he got back into town. And so, as Peter drove, I read. By the time we returned home three days later, I was ready to hang up my hamburgers for good. We bought a heavy-duty juicer, became connoisseurs of carrot juice, and loaded our refrigerator with fresh fruits and vegetables.

PHYSICAL HEALING

After adopting our new lifestyle in 1999, we noticed a feeling of wellness and a surge of energy along with clarity of mind and the healing of several minor physical ailments. We eventually settled on a largely vegan diet, including lots of fresh, living fruits and vegetables. Our goal was to reconstruct our bodies into uninviting hosts for cancers and other diseases.

I still had to deal with my pap smear results, though, so I anxiously went to the doctor for my treatment. Then, over the next six months, I waited to find out if the precancerous cells would return. I thank God they did not.

For Peter, who loves to cook, our diet and lifestyle adjustments inspire him in many ways. I often find him in the kitchen working on new recipes. As a TV producer, I see his mental wheels turning in the direction of cooking shows about this lifesaving cuisine. For my children, I know it will lead them into healthier and happier adulthood. As for me personally, I'm heading in the direction Jean Bertram and I prayed for—to be instrumental in helping others with the healing of their bodies and minds through exhortation in person and through my writing.

In 2003, Peter and I had the pleasure of meeting George Malkmus, and we thanked him personally for guiding us to a healthier way of life. Then, as an extra blessing from God, Peter and I were able to coauthor a book with Dr. Malkmus, *The Hallelujah Diet*. This book explains in great detail the cause-and-effect relationship between diet and health, offering a simple explanation of the diet and encouraging readers to regain their connections with their own bodies.

During those days I believe God was preparing our hearts and minds in many ways for the new road ahead of us. Our dreams for our family had changed. They involved moving in the direction of a more natural lifestyle—more nature, more family togetherness, less TV, less chemicals—in other words, less worldly.

ARE WE THERE YET?

Well, before I close this section of the book, I want to share a little story with you that will hopefully answer that question.

Occasionally our family climbs into the car—with a spirit of spur-of-the-moment adventures—and we go on a little voyage, staying overnight at a cabin or hotel somewhere not too far out of town. Usually our destination is no more than two to three hours away. To help occupy our minds and keep our stomachs quiet, we take along a few snacks, and the girls are never without books or their favorite stuffed animals. Then we settle back in our seats, ready for a change of scenery.

Almost always, within about thirty minutes, we hear little voices calling from the backseat: *"Are we there yet?"*

"In about two hours," I reply with a smile.

Ten minutes go by.

"When will we get there?" asks our youngest daughter, Grace.

"Soon, sweetie," I say, patiently. "We've still got about two hours to go. Just sit back and try to have fun."

"Okay," she says. We play a few games, count Volkswagens, then find the letters of the alphabet on signs or license plates. Fifteen minutes pass.

"Papa . . . Are we there yet?"

"Yes!" he says excitedly. "Just another *eight hours* and we'll be there!"

"Eight hours!" two voices yell from the back. "Paaa-paaa . . . Before, you said it was only two hours!"

"Well, all good things take time," Peter says with a twinkle in his eyes. "So you might as well sit back and enjoy the ride!"

I've always figured that to be pretty good advice on both our little trips and on our larger life journeys. Although I'll admit, sitting still and waiting are not always easy for me to do. Many times I have found myself working inside the house, cloaked in ever-growing darkness, striving to get further ahead and wondering if I can get everything done, while outside an extraordinary sunset is displayed without me.

But we humans are changeable, and over the last few years I've been making an effort do less living in the future—*Are we there yet?*—and more staring out the window at the beautiful scenery. It really is a wonderful ride.

So there you have it! *Are we there yet?* Have we found all the answers to a happier, healthier life? No, not all the answers have come, but I pray we're on the right path. For me, life is a continual journey of Light and connectedness—a journey of learning to be of service, helping one's own family and community, and hopefully enjoying the ride along the way.

PART IV

CONNECTIONS
AND CONCLUSIONS

CHAPTER EIGHTEEN

POWER AND LIGHT
FOR THE JOURNEY

*[Jesus said,] "Believe Me that I am in the Father
and the Father is in Me. Otherwise, believe because
of the works themselves. I assure you: The one who
believes in Me will also do the works that I do. And
he will do even greater works than these, because I
am going to the Father. Whatever you ask in My
name, I will do it so that the Father may be
glorified in the Son. If you ask Me anything
in My name, I will do it."*

—JOHN 14:11–14 HCSB

Peter

After witnessing Stowe's amazing healing from suppressed childhood memories, I had to take a new look at the subject of miracles, especially the topic of hands-on healing. I believe Jean Bertram's prayer for Stowe's rash was actually one step of a healing process that God had begun much earlier in Stowe's life, and I have to recognize that Jean had been led to us at the precise moment my wife needed that healing touch.

If we can imagine God's Light as healing energy on a journey, trying to complete its circuit between Him to us and back to Him by way of other people, then the very act of physical contact is a vital connection in that completed circuit.

Because we included stories of miraculous healings in the programs I produced for The Learning Channel and the Hallmark Channel, we knew we naturally studied the biblical accounts in which Jesus and His disciples performed amazing feats of healing the blind, the lame, and those with illnesses like leprosy. Then we interviewed several contemporary people who claim to have either been healed, or have performed healing on others, for both physical and emotional ailments.

A TOUCH THAT HEALS

One notable similarity between the Gospel accounts and the contemporary accounts we heard is the simple act of touch. Jesus always touches the people He heals, and His followers do, too—urging one another to lay hands upon the sick.

Today many alternative health care practitioners offer what is sometimes called *healing touch,* or energy work. I realize some eyebrows may rise at the mention of some of these practices, but I feel it is important to examine these phenomena that go beyond the norm. After all, Jesus was dealing with something far beyond everyday understanding when He healed the sick, and it is entirely possible that what He began is being continued in areas we have ignored or written off as strange.

In my own studies, I try to discern the spiritual source of the healing energy. If I discover that so-called healers are giving credit to God, or acknowledging the Spirit of Christ as the source of the healing energy, then I tend to believe this is coming from a reliable source. If, on the other hand, they ascribe the healing power to a spiritual deity that does *not* acknowledge Christ, or the One God and Creator, then I don't tend to look further. The Gospel writer John (son of Zebedee) was the apostle whom Jesus loved and who wrote more about the spiritual nature of Christ's Light than any of his peers. He was personally involved with deeply spiritual phenomena, eventually culminating in the vision he wrote as the Book of Revelation. John wrote the following advice to believers who were drawn to spiritual phenomena and teachings that were floating around the early church:

> Dear friends, do not believe every spirit, but test the spirits to see whether they are from God, because many false prophets have gone out into the world. This is how you can recognize the Spirit of God. Every spirit that acknowledges that Jesus Christ has come in the flesh is from God, but every spirit that does not acknowledge Jesus is not from God. (1 J O H N 4 : 1 – 3 N I V)

Many of today's self-professed healers describe incorporating a combination of prayer and physical touch to locate weaknesses in a person's *electrical energy,* so to speak. This energy—sometimes called bioenergy—resides, as I generally understand the Eastern concept, within the body's chakras, or energy centers, which correspond to the location of the endocrine glands. According to the strength or weakness in that "energy field," which practitioners learn to perceive as a kind of heat, they will then put their own hands on or near that area in order to help strengthen the energy field of the patient. This sounds to me like jump-starting a battery for a stranded motorist and implies that God's healing energy (or Spirit) might flow from one person to another, as through an electrical contact or connection.

Stowe

Before we share some of the stories from people who have been the benefactors of God's kind of *healing energy,* let's examine some of the bigger questions people have about miraculous healing.

THE BIG QUESTIONS ABOUT HEALING

Has the *miraculous healing power* that God exhibited more than two thousand years ago become just a mythical memory in today's world? Or are there contemporary people who are regularly touched by genuine spiritual healing from afflictions, such as the kinds Jesus treated: blindness, birth defects, mental or emotional illness, and otherwise incurable diseases?

If Jesus' claim is true—*that He really would bestow His healing gift to those who followed in His footsteps*—then shouldn't that gift be evident in a world populated with His followers? Doesn't Jesus' declaration provide clues to one of humanity's greatest untapped resources, and isn't it worthy of great study and inquiry? And if it is true, then don't those who profess to be Christ's disciples have a responsibility to allow that power to manifest itself through their daily lives?

God knows this world is at a critical crossroads, and surviving the coming era will take all of His miraculous healing power we can muster.

The apostle John once again recorded an amazing spiritual challenge by quoting Jesus as saying: *"I tell you the truth, anyone who has faith in me will do what I have been doing. They will do even greater things than these, because I am going to the Father"* (John 14:12 NIV).

What was Jesus imagining when He delivered this amazing prophecy about miracle-working to His disciples? Can you:

- imagine a civilization filled with Christlike miracle workers, each exhibiting the power that caused such excitement in the first century?
- imagine a neighborhood where the father of three who lives next door contracts cancer and the woman across the street is called to lay healing hands on the afflicted area?
- imagine a city street where a babbling homeless woman is not ignored, but rather is approached by a discerning couple that commands a confused spirit to leave the body, which that spirit has made a home?
- imagine a nation where doctors and research hospitals focus mainly on preventive health, because an abundance of spiritual healers have supplanted traditional medicine?
- imagine a time when the human race has advanced to a level of love for one another—a time when sensitivity to God's Spirit is shared by the majority?

Could these scenarios possibly be what Christ envisioned? If what Jesus spoke about was possible, then shouldn't miracles be commonplace in this world? It is indeed hard to find such proof in our culture today, if all the evidence we gathered to prove Christ's prophecy were to come from the majority of self-professing Christians in Western civilization. I realize this is a very challenging topic, but it is one we really must come to terms with.

HEALING MIRACLES IN
OUR WORLD TODAY

One out of six persons in the world today would mark "Christian" on the birth certificate of their newborn child. But that inheritance does not typically supply much miraculous power with it, when you consider the relative scarcity of Christlike healing in the Christianized societies of today. The issue of modern-day miracles is irritating, to say the least, to many people's professed worldview. It is shrugged off by those who absolutely *do not* believe Jesus performed the miracles written about in the Gospels. And it is disturbing, too, for many who *do* believe He performed miracles—but who rationalize that those powers were reserved exclusively for the Son of God, and maybe a few of His early disciples—but are certainly not expected to be performed today by regular folk. I believe the scarcity of powerful miracles in the lives of many Christians today is *not due to any lack of God's ability*. Quite the contrary! I think it has more to do with the *lack of people's expectations*.

In Third World countries where people's expectations are not bound by science or materialism, we hear stories from missionaries of amazing miracles that are like stories out of the first century. Perhaps a major study needs to be done on this very subject. I suspect that faith and expectations are simply more academic in the civilized Western world, and we don't allow the Spirit enough room to work.

Peter

I have never been too interested in Religion with a big "R." Sacred doctrines without Spirit are like a house with no electric-ity—dark and empty. I am a follower of Christ because I know His Spirit is *alive*. I know that He is alive because He touched me in a perceivable way, through the realm of the Spirit. And I know that His power is still active because of the evidence I constantly see. But the most vivid sign of His presence—as evident today as when He walked the earth—is the extraordinary healing that He performs; it seems linked directly to His relationship to the force of *life* itself. And He offers a clear picture of how and why *He can perform healing through us, and through the people whom we touch.*

I have witnessed and experienced the gift of miraculous healing, but I was still forced to take inventory of my sacred beliefs when I saw the gift in action with Stowe's foster mother, Judy McDonald.

JUDY McDONALD

Judy was suffering terribly from a liver ailment that caused her constant pain and discomfort. Doctors were unable to help, and Judy was losing hope. One weekend Stowe and I visited her in Greenville, South Carolina.

As we discussed her ailment, I mentioned a book whose author I was interviewing for a film. It turned out that Judy had also read and was deeply moved by the book, which portrays Jesus' eternal power over life, death, and sickness. To lift Judy's spirits, I phoned the author and asked if she would please say hello to my wife's sick mother. Judy was beside herself, and they chatted on the phone for a good while.

After hanging up, Judy was radiant and asked if we would pray with her for healing. We gladly agreed, and Stowe and I placed our hands on Judy's abdomen. We prayed that the same One who healed the sick and raised the dead so long ago would please make her liver clean and well.

When we finished, Judy cried and said she felt warmth . . . but no more pain! She hasn't had a day of discomfort since, and to this day, many years later, the doctors say her liver is completely well.[1]

Believe it or not, after what I witnessed with Judy, I was still a *bit* of a Doubting Thomas and scratched my head over that incident for a long time. Like those whom Christ called "ye of little faith," I have not fully ventured to tap God's power nearly often enough, especially in the way we did for Judy that day. *Why not?* I believe my logical mind is probably just too stubborn to let His overwhelming power take control. So, like many nominal Christians, I hover instead in a safely uncommitted state of *not expecting* too many ground-shaking miracles. Yet, when I hear stories and testimonials of other people's healing episodes, then my own faith is bolstered and, like Judy, I can muster up the courage to *actually ask* for a miracle. This is confirmed by Jesus' frequent message to those whom He healed: "Your *faith* has made you well." I believe we need to not only have faith, but we need to be bold enough to take the initiative to touch other people and *pray,* even when we're wary of the results.

Stowe

Peter's associate producer on *Miracles, Angels & Afterlife* is a remarkable man named Fred Rowles. Earlier in this book there is a story of healing for our good friend Linda. She was paired with Fred in that healing workshop, and now we want to share Fred's story with you.

Although Fred had spent nearly thirty years as a documentary producer for United Methodist Communications, he was not a typical coat-and-tie guy—a refreshing change from the businesslike atmosphere of UMCom. He had investigated Christian mysticism around the world and collected ethnic trinkets from his travels to nearly fifty countries during the production of dozens of missionary films. Fred was perfectly suited to work on the extraordinary stories often covered in the TV series he produced with Peter.

These two men knew the Lord meant for them to work side by side, like peas in a pod, as soon as their executive producer put them together. They laughed aloud the day they were introduced as they realized how closely their career paths had overlapped in thirty years, coincidentally, with many associates across the country in common. In fact, they discovered that they had each had their very first job at the same small film studio in Baltimore, Maryland.

Many months later they were still trying to laugh when Fred got a bad work review one day for being "too spiritual." It seemed an ironic comment coming from a church-related organization. Peter knew how much it hurt Fred, even though he brushed it aside and continued doing what he felt God had called him to do.

Fred was particularly interested in stories they covered about spiritual healing, and we eventually discovered the reason for his interest. Several years earlier an experience had "turned his lights on" (literally) to the idea of miraculous healing energy.

ARCH ANTHONY DAWSON

In 1992, Fred and his wife Ruthie received a call that her father, Arch Anthony Dawson, who lived in California, was in the hospital with renal kidney failure. The family was faced with the decision to take Arch off dialysis and let nature take its course. But nobody was comfortable with making that choice for the unconscious man.

As it happened, Arch soon awoke and made his own decision to be removed from life support. The doctors predicted he would not live more than three or four days.

Fred was very fond of his father-in-law, whom he regarded as his own dad, and agonized over the idea of losing him. On the day the machines were turned off, he forced himself outside for his daily jog; as he often did, Fred prayed while he ran. Fred says that ordinarily he would pray only for a cure. This time, however, he found himself saying a different prayer.

"God, I'm not going to ask You to cure Arch. . . ." Fred recalls praying. "I trust You in my heart, for whatever You will do. If he dies, I'm at peace with that. If he lives, I'm at peace with that, too."

Fred later said, "I literally gave it to God, saying, 'I trust You.' "

"And then something strange happened," Fred continued, "and I hope nobody thinks I'm a fruitcake for saying this . . . but all of a sudden, in my mind's eye, I saw my hands stretch out . . . kind of like Superman. I saw my hands moving toward California. I could see the ground passing below. . . ." Fred rolled his eyes upward while recalling this vision, obviously worrying about how it sounded to me.

"Then I saw my hands fly into the hospital . . . into my

father-in-law's room . . . grab hold of his hands . . . and then I saw this green light flowing. It was flowing through my hands, into his arms, and into his body. The light filled up my father-in-law's body completely . . . filled up the entire room . . . and then it was over. By that time, I had run twice as far as I usually ran, losing total track of where I was."

Fred returned home and entered the house saying, "Ruthie, your father isn't going to die." He proceeded to tell her about his vision because he wanted it to go on record. Then they waited.

Four days later they still hadn't heard anything and said to each other, "This is ridiculous! We should have heard something by now!" Fred then called the hospital desk for news, and he got a baffled reply. "Well, Mr. Rowles, we don't know exactly what happened, but four days ago when we took Arch off dialysis his kidneys started working again. Oh, the doctor still expects him to die. There is really no chance of recovery."

At that, Fred says he started laughing and said to the nurse, "I'll be flying to California in about a week, and I'll have a story to tell you and the doctor." When they arrived a week later, Ruthie's father was sitting up, his kidneys still functioning normally. Fred told his story to the doctor, who nodded and said, "Well, sure, that's very nice. But you understand, don't you, he's still going to die?"

One year later, the hospital staff held a celebration for Arch. After the party, the same doctor looked at Fred and said, "I don't know what happened, but it isn't of this world. I believe you now."

Arch lived for another eight years, and eventually did die . . . of a heart attack.[2]

Peter

When I was a young man of fourteen, I experienced what I call a Christ encounter. I believe it was what Jesus called *being reborn*. It was unexpected, and profoundly spiritual.

I have since understood that there is a vast difference between the God of empty religious doctrine and the vibrant God by whom Christ was empowered. One God lives as myth—the other as a vital spirit. One God derives power from people's interpretation of other people's beliefs—one is the *source of power* by which everyone and everything in the universe exists.

My experience happened within the religious context of Chevy Chase Baptist Church, in the suburbs of Washington, D.C. The fact that it was a Baptist church isn't particularly significant. What was important was the contrast between the two types of God that one could find there. Like in many churches, there was a sleepy section of the congregation that attended religiously to worship a seemingly mythical God—a God who received the people's offerings and then watched them return to their sometimes hypocritical and judgmental, however righteous, lives. There were also a significant number of people who truly loved and worshiped the God of the second sort—a living, vibrant God who loved and listened to His children. You could tell the two groups apart by the depth of love they had for other people.

The minister, Rev. Richard E. Drehmer, was one of the latter group, and he introduced me to the God of true spiritual power.

DICK DREHMER

When Dick was a little boy, he had experienced a miracle. His family lived in Corning, New York, and his parents were God-loving people. One day, five-year-old Dick fell horribly ill and was rushed to the local hospital. He was diagnosed with acute appendicitis and was immediately admitted for emergency surgery. After the operation, Dr. Whipple, an amiable old country physician, came out to break the bad news to his parents. "I'm very sorry, but your boy's appendix had already ruptured before arriving at the hospital. Peritonitis and gangrene have set in . . . I'm afraid he won't last through the night."

Dick's parents told Dr. Whipple they believed their son was in God's hands, and they wouldn't stop praying for him. The doctor said, "I wish I had your faith. Personally, I'm an agnostic. I just don't think we can know whether there is a God. But I hope, for your son's sake, that if there is a God, he hears your prayers."

Dick's dad rushed to the church to gather up the men's prayer band, a circle of gentlemen who assembled for just such emergencies. Those men held up the young Drehmer boy in their prayers all night until the sun rose the next morning.

In the morning, Dick's parents hurried back to the hospital to check on him. The old doctor met the parents outside the hospital room door with a furrowed brow and said, "Your son is alive. Not because of anything I did. *Your God did this.*"[3]

Dick's experience showed me that we need to put our faith to work. His mom and dad had taught him how to do it, and he passed it on to others like me. Despite terrifying hardships and when there seems to be no light at the end of the dark tunnel, God's Light continues its journey—from heart to heart to heart.

Stowe

Many years after Dick Drehmer told Peter the story of his childhood healing, Peter and I heard a story from another father of another sick little boy. Todd Beezley and his wife Sherry faced a family crisis that turned their worst fears into an opportunity for putting faith to the ultimate test.

JOSHUA BEEZLEY

Sherry Beezley stared curiously at the little "L" shape on the pregnancy indicator. It was not exactly the *plus* sign she had been hoping for, but it wasn't a *minus* sign either. For eighteen long years she and her husband Todd had been trying without success to conceive. Now she anxiously wondered, *Could it really be true?* A visit to the doctor confirmed her hunch. The Beezleys were finally going to have a baby!

As far as the happy couple was concerned, this was nothing short of a miracle. Sherry and Todd, both thirty-eight years old, had all but given up the dream of having a natural family. In fact, they had already looked into adoption; but now the two were busy making preparations for the new arrival. It seemed like things were finally falling into place.

Only one dark cloud hung in their happy sky: Todd had been born with an inherited condition known as osteogenesis imperfecta, better known as brittle bone disease. It is a condition that affects children, robbing its young victims of the precious calcium their bones need. Without this vital mineral, the child is as fragile as a china doll. They must be gently carried for years until they can walk on their own. Their childhood is often a lonely one, spent on the sidelines of life: no games or sports, no activity that might risk a broken bone. Often by the age of puberty, though, chemical changes in the body allow many sufferers to begin absorbing the calcium missing from their skeleton. With age, bone problems begin to decrease in frequency and severity.

The Beezleys genetics counselor had warned them that there was a 50 percent chance their child might inherit Todd's disease. Knowing this, Todd found himself haunted by the memories of his own childhood: the painful broken bones, the string of hospitals, and the surgeries. He had suffered through no less than twenty-eight broken bones and corrective surgeries in his lifetime. His brother, Gary, who also had the disease, was hospitalized ten times. Todd was understandably anxious about his unborn child. *Oh, God*, he prayed, *please don't let our child have my disease.*

The Beezleys also asked others to pray. Todd recalls, "We asked friends all the way from Virginia to California to pray with us for two things: that our new baby would come to love the Lord with all its heart at an early age, and that he or she would be born without my birth defect." And then they waited.

Finally the big day arrived, and Joshua was born; but one look at the tiny infant shattered Todd and Sherry's hopes for a healthy baby. Joshua had obviously inherited the dreaded birth defect. "We were totally devastated," says Todd. In the delivery room, Sherry longed to hold her newborn baby. Instead, he was whisked away from her. From across the room, she strained for a glimpse of him through the flurry of doctors and nurses attending him. But the sight of Joshua only broke her heart. The nurses were administering oxygen to his tiny lifeless and blue body. Sherry felt her dreams of being a mother slipping away once again. *How could God allow this to happen? Have we come all this way just to have our son die?*

Joshua began to stabilize. Then complete X-rays were made of him. They showed almost no bone at the back of his skull, his ribs crossed over one another, and his little legs were badly bent. Blood tests confirmed that Joshua's calcium level was far too high, which meant the calcium would pass through his bloodstream and out of his body, leaving his bones brittle. No amount of calcium supplements would ever be able to help treat the disease or strengthen Joshua's bones during childhood.

But as terrible as this news was, Joshua had another, far more serious problem threatening his life. Due to a miscalculated conception date, Joshua had been born by Caesarean three weeks early. Doctors informed the Beezleys that their son's lungs were not fully developed. Unable to take in oxygen, his chances of survival were slim. His only hope lay in getting him to a critical care newborn ICU unit.

Todd watched helplessly as Joshua struggled for each breath. Choking back tears, he held his son's tiny fingers and whispered good-bye, possibly for the last time. Joshua was then rushed to a regional hospital thirty-five miles away.

Alone in the darkness of her hospital room, Sherry fell into a deep depression. "I felt as though my life had ended," she says. "I did pray but I felt my prayers were weak. It seemed God was far away. . . . Still, somehow I knew He was there."

Back at home, Todd, too, began to pray. Mixed with his prayers, however, was the nagging question, *Why? Why does my son have this birth defect?* Todd remembers feeling disappointed, almost betrayed, by God. So Todd searched the Bible for answers. One scripture he found comfort in vowed "the son shall live." Todd was overcome with emotion. *This is an incredibly powerful message, but is it really true?* He clung tightly to the hope it brought him, and he immediately went to work calling friends, asking them to pray for Joshua's healing. Throughout the weekend Todd felt assured that Joshua would make it.

The days following Joshua's birth were a roller-coaster ride of emotions featuring improvements and medical setbacks. At one point there was even a diagnosis of a heart condition, which, fortunately, was found not to exist. Finally, eleven days after Joshua's birth, he was released to his parents without aid of a baby monitor or medication. Todd took it as a confirmation: "Just as promised, the son did live!"

The months passed and Joshua slowly grew. As fragile as a little eggshell, his cautious parents carried him everywhere. At eighteen months, however, he began trying to stand up for the first time. With a great show of determination, Joshua would pull himself up on the baby gate, his bent legs wobbling under the strain. After a few seconds, though, he would slump down into a little ball and cry. This scene repeated itself many times and tore at the hearts of both his parents.

Several days later, an out-of-state friend called to tell them about a man he knew who lived in Ohio, a man who was a believer in miraculous healing. This man had prayed for the friend's wife, who had been healed of a leg problem. Todd's friend gave him the man's phone number. Todd recalls, "I had nothing to lose so I made the call."

"It was one of the most wonderful, awe-inspiring experiences of my life," says Todd. "This total stranger asked me by phone to lay hands on Joshua and to agree with him in prayer. Then, through what this man claimed as the power of the Holy Spirit, he told me everything I already knew was wrong with my son, including some things I did not know, and one thing that only God could have known!"

Todd recalls the man saying, "Your son has flat feet. We're praying for that. He has a bent ankle. We're praying for that."

"One by one," Todd says, "he identified all Joshua's symptoms and prayed for God to touch and heal our son. He correctly described a knee being angled out improperly, a vertebra out of place near the base of Joshua's spine, a misshapen pelvis that was putting pressure on his bladder (which I did not know about), a pinched sciatica nerve to his left leg, and most amazingly of all, he said, 'Your son has too much calcium in his bone marrow.' The neonatal doctor had indeed told us our son had too much calcium in his bloodstream, and no one except the doctor, my wife, and God knew that part of the diagnosis. We had never been told it is the bone marrow that helps produce the blood cells, and I later found out that was a very perceptive diagnosis. Clearly, God was at work. The man closed his prayer with, 'We'll just believe God for a good report.' "

Three days later, an astonished but happy mother and father watched their son triumphantly stand up in the middle of the living room floor for the first time.

One week later the Beezleys took Joshua to the bone specialist for his eighteen-month checkup. After careful examination of the little boy's body, the doctor said, "He looks great."

Todd asked hesitantly, "But what about the curvatures in his legs?"

"What curvatures?" the doctor replied. "I see kids in here all the time who don't have your son's condition, and Joshua has less curvature in his legs than they do."

Todd and Sherry were ecstatic; they could hardly contain

their excitement. But it wasn't until several days later that they found the medical proof of what God had already accomplished.

The Beezleys had taken a trip to west Tennessee to visit the dairy farm where Sherry's father worked. Soon after arriving, Sherry decided to show Joshua the cows. Picking up her son, she headed toward the pasture. But while walking across the yard, Sherry stepped into a hole and twisted her ankle. As they fell, Joshua hit his head on the ground. He immediately began crying uncontrollably and throwing up. Joshua was rushed to Humboldt General Hospital for X-rays. Amazingly there were no concussions or fractures.

Curious about the general condition of Joshua's bones, Todd couldn't help but ask the radiologist how Joshua's bones looked. Joshua had never been exposed to the unnecessary radiation of routine X-rays during his entire eighteen months of life, so as Todd and the radiologist beheld the first X-ray of Joshua since the day he was born, the miraculous healing was there in black and white.

Whereas Joshua's natal X-ray had revealed almost no bone at the back of his skull . . . the new one showed that the bone had completely grown into place! The tiny ribs that Todd and Sherry had seen crossing over one another on their son's first X-ray were now totally straightened. "The technician," Todd says happily, "told me Joshua's bones looked like those of a normal eighteen-month-old."

Within one month of that powerful and life-changing prayer, Joshua was strong enough to begin walking by himself. After two months he was up and running. When he was taken in for his nineteen-month bone doctor visit, the doctor concluded, "Well, he still has flat feet. He'll need to wear shoes with arch supports. Other than that, don't bother bringing him back to see me again." Then he quipped, "You'd be wasting my time and your money."

Todd and Sherry later watched in wonder as six-year-old Joshua darted happily about the backyard, occasionally taking tumbles that would have sent Todd to the hospital when he was that age. Todd, who still suffers the aftereffects of his own brittle bone condition, is currently wearing an ankle brace and walking with crutches. He relates, "I have not been able to catch up with Joshua since his healing, and it's the most wonderful problem in the world!"

Todd will never forget his own anguished childhood; yet he begins to understand his suffering in the context of all that has happened. "God had everything in control. He was there and was in charge, even when Joshua was born with my birth defect." As Sherry now says, "God was building our faith. He wanted us to see His supernatural healing power at work."[4]

The Beezleys were allowed to take an amazing journey, one that spanned the course of two generations. God's power was revealed in an unmistakable way through the prayer of a stranger for their son.

Their faith is now of the unshakable kind. They know just how deeply God cares about His children—and how He knows when we're in trouble and how He hears us when we cry out from our hearts. They know firsthand about the connection between prayer and the power of the Holy Spirit.

CHAPTER NINETEEN

CONDUITS OF GOD'S
HEALING LIGHT

In the same way the Spirit also helps our weakness;
for we do not know how to pray as we should,
but the Spirit Himself intercedes for us with
groanings too deep for words.
—ROM. 8:26 NASB

Stowe

Part of the adventure of any journey is looking back to see some of the roads you've traveled—the ups, the downs, and some of the miraculous "chance meetings" you've had. Remembering how you got to where you are now is sometimes difficult, but those special people you meet along the way make the journey worthwhile.

We have experienced such awe and thankfulness while hearing people tell us their stories of how they or their loved ones have been healed. That grateful feeling is only matched by the stories we gathered from people who are not only the *healed* but the *healers*—selfless individuals connected with God on some rudimentary level that allows them to "patch in" as conduits of God's healing energy. Three of the people we'll look at are Jean Bertram, Tricia McMahon, and Sharon Forrest.

JEAN

Earlier I told you about Jean Bertram, the woman who prayed for the terrible rash on my hands and arms. This is the story of how we came to know her.

The first time Jean called our house she was afraid Peter would be a little skeptical of her. "I know this is going to sound kinda crazy," Jean told him, "but I was reading your book, *Reflections of Heaven,* this morning, and every time I picked it up I heard a voice say to me, 'Call him.' Well, this went on for about five hours, and I tried everything to put the voice out of my mind. I thought, *There's no way a published author would have his phone number listed.* But because I felt God was leading me, I called directory assistance. Within minutes I had your number. So, here I am! I really don't have the faintest idea of what I'm supposed to do now."

Peter laughed and said, "Well, let's just talk a little bit and see if we can figure it out."

Within minutes Peter had told her about these chapters on healing that we were about to begin writing. That's when they made the connection. Jean professes a gift in the area of healing and has been active with it for the last fourteen years. "Aha!" they both agreed. "That's why we've been put together."

On the surface the book did seem like the perfect reason for us to meet Jean Bertram but, as is often the case, God had further-reaching goals than any of us could understand.

You've read the chapter openers for this book, so you know how divinely God has touched my life through Jean. But what none of us can know, at least not in this lifetime, are the ways in which that small miracle will touch others.

It's amazing how God chose Jean, a woman with a childhood of sexual abuse, to drive two and a half hours to our house and speak to us for six hours about her broken childhood while I was suffering from the same kinds of wounds. One of today's popular proverbs goes "All you have to do is *let go and let God*." But as Jean Bertram will tell you, "It's not always that easy." Here is the story of how she responded when *she* got the call:

Jean has always been a spiritual woman, believing strongly in God's power. She has felt God's presence in her life since she was a small child. Over the years, she says, the Lord has given her visions—the ability to interpret dreams and a gift of discernment; quite often she seems to just "know" things about people. Why she has been given these gifts is a mystery to her, but Jean is sure of the source. Even so, she has not always been comfortable with these abilities and, for the most part, has sought to conceal them.

However, in the spring of 1986, Jean began her journey of learning that God's Light is much too powerful to be hidden under a basket.

In the little town of Fayetteville, North Carolina, the Sunday morning streets were still. A soft, melodic hymn wafted from the open windows of the small Catalpa Baptist Church where Jean Bertram was a member of the congregation. The preaching for that day was done; now it was time for the invitation—a part of the service where a few who feel the need can heed the pastor's call to come down to the altar for prayer.

Jean watched with interest as a mother and her wheelchair-bound son made their way down the aisle. She had seen them before. In fact, they were there every Sunday, and almost every week the mother wheeled her son to the front for prayer. Jean had the feeling the mother was not bringing her son down simply for healing. Somehow Jean knew it was the mother's guilt over her son's paralysis that drove her to the altar each week. Jean continued studying them from her pew.

Suddenly a powerful voice commanded her, "Lay your hands on him and heal him."

Taken by surprise, Jean spun around in her pew. *Who said that?* she wondered. The voice sounded as though it had come from behind her. Looking left and then right, she noticed the people surrounding her all had their heads bowed in prayer. *Okay,* she thought, *I'm really losing it now.*

Then the voice came again: "Lay your hands on him and heal him."

By now there was no doubt in Jean's mind that this was the voice of God. She couldn't help but wonder, though, if He had made a mistake in calling on her. "I can't heal anybody," she argued desperately. "You are talking to the wrong person, Lord!"

And then she heard these words: "No, you can't heal him, but I can through you. Lay your hands on this child."

Jean's heart raced. Panic set in. She recalls thinking, *This is a little "out there," even for me.* Struggling for understanding, she questioned God. Was He really asking her to perform a miracle? What would people think if she told them she was going to lay her hands on someone? What if she got everyone's hopes raised—only to be dashed by failure? Jean hated to question the Almighty, but what if nothing happened?

Confused and frightened, she left the church and hurried home. In the safety of her room, she looked through her Bible. Jean says, "I knew in my spirit that the Lord was going to heal the boy, but it terrified me. Even though I had read in the Bible about how God had made lame men walk, I couldn't help but think, *That happened back then . . . not today!*"

A month passed, and Jean tried to put the incident out of

her mind; but it was impossible. The woman and her son Allen lived only two blocks from Jean. Each day, on her way to and from work, Jean would hear the message, "Lay your hands on him." Stubbornly, she clung to the belief that God had somehow made a mistake. "Who am *I* to perform miracles?" she reasoned. "I can't even take care of myself." But as time went by, Jean felt the Spirit breaking down her resistance. Still afraid, she began promising, "I'll do it tomorrow, Lord."

One night as she drifted off to sleep, Jean had a vision. In it, she saw herself and Allen's mother going into his bedroom. With Allen in bed, both Jean and the mother laid their hands on him and prayed.

The next evening as Jean made her way home from work, she again heard the familiar voice say, "This is the last time I will tell you. Go lay your hands on him. Will you do that for Me? Will you just trust Me and go?"

Jean gave in. "Okay, Lord," she said. "I'll go."

Taking a deep breath, Jean summoned her courage and knocked on the apartment door. Allen's mother greeted her, beer in hand. Entering the living room, Jean saw the woman's boyfriend, also drinking a beer. Jean braced herself—*This isn't going to be easy*. How would she explain why she was here? Jean decided to "just say it." She told the woman about what had happened in the church and also shared with her the vision from the night before. "I don't know what the Lord wants to do," Jean explained to her. "But I know I've got to lay my hands on your son."

Allen's mother listened patiently, then informed Jean that she had tried everything to help her son, all to no avail. Doctors had told her for years that her son would never walk. Intrigued by Jean's story, however, she did agree to let her pray for him. But before Jean could begin, she swore the woman to secrecy. "If the Lord heals your child," she whispered, "you cannot tell a soul that it was me who came and laid my hands on him, okay?" Jean was still too uncertain about the strong compulsion she was now submitting to. The woman promised to keep the secret.

Within minutes Jean was kneeling beside Allen's bed, laying her hands on him. Her prayer for the child was short. Her vision of the night before was fulfilled. Jean felt she had been faithful—she had shown up, and she had prayed. Now it was time for God to work His wonders.

A week later Jean was drawn to the bold headlines of the local newspaper: NEW REHABILITATION CENTER OPENS—BOY WALKS! Her heart pounded as she stared at the large photograph of Allen, who was pictured walking between parallel bars. Jean saw him in church the next Sunday, out of his wheelchair and walking without any help! Completely stunned, Jean says, "I was just so blown away, and I kept thinking, *He did it! God did it!*" And she marveled in the fact that He had chosen her to be a part of it.

Personally, when listening to Jean tell her story, I wondered why the newspaper hadn't mentioned her prayer. "The only thing I regret now," Jean says, "is that God didn't get the glory because I swore that mother to secrecy. But, I really wasn't ready to handle the attention. It did teach me, though, that Jesus is alive and well, and that God does care."

With all the excitement that Allen's miracle created within her, Jean began having fears about her own future as a healer. "I started wondering, *What do I do now? Should I go up to the hospital and go room to room and lay my hands on everybody who's sick?*"

Jean began having dreams of opening her front door and seeing scores of people waiting to be healed, and all she could think was, *What if I can't help them?* "It's not that I doubted God," she says, "it's that I doubted myself. Who am I to choose who lives or dies or is healed or not healed?" Deep inside, Jean knew her thoughts were not always His thoughts, and she worried, *What if I don't agree with Him?*

And so it was quite a while before Jean would lay her hands on anyone else. "If I prayed for anyone, I would do it in my prayer closet," she says, "because I was afraid of what was in my hands." But over the years Jean has felt God urging her, almost pushing her at times, to lay her hands on people. And each time she obeyed, she has seen the miraculous healing God had in store for the people she touched. She says, "I would know within my spirit when it was time, and I finally learned to trust Him—*He* knows best. And I learned that the greatest motivator, the basis for all His blessings, is *love*."[1]

Peter

I was introduced to a woman who performs a treatment she calls *healing touch*. Tricia, like several other professed healers we've met, says she became aware of the gift when she was a child. She would pray for people, laying hands on them, and they would feel better.

TRICIA

In adulthood, during a difficult time of life—recently divorced and raising small children—Tricia was diagnosed with spinosis, in which the nerves in her spine were being constricted by narrowing channels in the vertebrae and leaving her in crippling pain. Her doctors recommended surgery to drill out the channels in her spine. A friend suggested that before such invasive surgery, she first see a *healing touch* practitioner. During the session, Tricia felt something familiar happening to her—a tingling sensation, like that which she felt while praying for others as a child. The results were so dramatic that she elected not to have surgery, much to her medical doctor's chagrin.

After her own complete healing, Tricia heard a strong inner voice saying, "Call St. Thomas Hospital and ask if they need a Eucharistic minister," which is a layman who volunteers to serve communion to those who can't attend church.

Tricia was interviewed by Father Campbell at a local parish, and after reviewing her responses to a list of questions, he replied, "Well, you *are* a Eucharistic minister!"

Still in doubt over her new calling, she recalls going in tears to the hospital for the first time, saying to herself, *I can't do this!* She then heard the inner voice again, saying, "That's right, *you* can't! But God can!" She remembers walking through the corridors with her head lowered, " the way I remember seeing nuns doing, to avoid having eye contact with anyone. I was so afraid my personality would get in the way, and that I would lose my humility." But she says she felt God reassuring her that if her heart was right, she would remain humble.

Touching is not usually a part of the job description of a Eucharist minister; however, while serving communion to patients in the hospital, Tricia bent the rules by asking if they wished for her to pray and lay hands on them. She became aware that something tangible was being transferred between her and the patients. She was frequently asked by the patients, "What was that?" or, "What is *that tingling* feeling?"

Tricia went to a priest to find out what was really going on, and he told her it was just her imagination and not to talk about it because people might think she was crazy. But she continued to inquire, and an older priest replied simply, "Oh, don't worry about it, that's just the Holy Spirit!" She felt affirmed and sought to learn more. She found a group that taught a technique called *healing touch*, which she felt was akin to her own experiences. Her confidence grew and so did the number of successes to her efforts.

Gradually the nurses and doctors began realizing that Tricia's visits were causing marked improvement in a number of their patients. She was surprised that, rather than being put off, the medical staff welcomed her healing touch as a form of therapy. They felt that if it helped the patients, it was a positive thing, even if they couldn't explain it scientifically.

The greatest affirmation came one afternoon when she was administering healing touch to a patient, and an anesthesiologist entered the room to do his work. He said to Tricia, respectfully, "Oh, excuse me. . . . I don't want to get in your way!"

Today Tricia's contacts are regularly referred to her by doctors from St. Thomas Hospital and Baptist Hospital, two major medical centers in Nashville. On several occasions she has been invited to perform her work on patients during surgery. Tricia is frequently asked to write her comments in patients' medical charts, a step that further validates her work. She also conducts sessions privately in her home office.

When talking with doctors who are curious about her methods, she explains the process as providing deep relaxation to the autonomic nervous system. "Increasing the flow of energy in the nervous system helps optimize the body's ability to heal itself."

One doctor recently replied, "Okay, but can you please explain this to me scientifically without using the word 'energy'?"

"All right," Tricia answered. "In the oriental practice of

acupuncture," which Western medicine has acknowledged as an alternative therapy, though not fully understood, "the concept of the meridian zones describes a kind of circuitry that runs throughout the body. These meridians conduct the flow of an electrical force, which the body needs in order to run properly. The circuits intersect at junctions, which acupuncturists call 'chakras,' corresponding directly to the location of the endocrine glands. When certain chakras are not working properly, then the electrical force doesn't flow fully and may cause poor health in the rest of the body. Acupuncture needles are introduced to help correct that flow of current." Trisha continued, "So this thing I call 'healing touch' is doing the same thing, but it uses the electrical field of another human being—ourselves—instead of using needles."

After hearing Tricia's explanation, I recalled other terms I have heard used to describe this kind of energy, such as the pseudoscientific *life force* or *bioenergy*, and words I heard in college yoga class like *chi* and *prajna*. Similarly, the Greek word *Zoë* is used in John's Gospel to describe Christ's Light as the *life of all people*, generally translating into English as the *divine spark of life*, or the vitality that animates life.

I asked Tricia to stretch the limits of my cultural language and explain to me how a person's energy can become unbalanced in the first place. She explained, "Like I told the doctor, our energy emits from these junctions called 'chakras,' or energy centers, in our central nervous system, which regulate the healthy flow of energy to various parts of the body. When a person goes through a trauma of some kind, say, a sexual trauma, it inhibits the corresponding energy center, which regulates not only sexual health, but many other bodily functions as well. If that emotional trauma remains unresolved, the person then develops a pattern of inhibition, which we call a 'blockage.' The blockage prevents the current from flowing normally from that center into other seemingly unrelated areas of the body that are also connected to that center."

When someone comes to Tricia with an ailment, she wants to know how far back in the person's life those symptoms started showing. She can often trace back the ailment to an emotional trauma, which corresponds to the energy center regulating the health of that ailing part of the body. Again, the connection between emotional causes and physical effects may not appear obvious, until considered in relation to the linkages in the body's circuitry.

Tricia gave a simple explanation of how healing can occur, by the release of pent-up emotions. She said, "Breaking an energetic pattern—what some practitioners call a *neuro-linguistic loop* in the mind—gives patients freedom to engage themselves with who they really are, spiritually, without having to cling to the past. So many people are holding onto their same old, sad life story, which they endlessly recite to themselves and to others. Often, a person can't be revitalized until they change the story they believe their life is all about. My job is to help people shed the past and begin a whole new chapter. In this way, healing is a gentle unfolding, allowing a new self-discovery."

I asked Tricia to describe exactly what perception she uses when trying to detect the condition of someone else's energy. She used the words *heat* and *tingling* to relate the sensation, and explained, "I have developed a sensitivity in which someone else's energy field becomes connected to my own, and I can actually pick up on what their energy pattern *feels* like." Compassion seems to play a big part in developing this kind of empathetic sensitivity. Tricia adds, "*Love* is another word to describe this healing energy we are working with. It is important to try to become an ego-less healer, because we have to tap into a place of unselfish compassion within us.

"I really don't feel like I am a healer. I think of it as God's work. I just wake up in the morning and show up! The real work is between the sick person and God."[2]

Stowe

You'll remember Sharon from Linda's healing experience. She says she began to experience healing miracles when she was a child, learning to trust that God would answer her prayers.

SHARON

Sharon says she has experienced so many incidents of miraculous healings that she has lost track of them. Although we had difficulty corroborating the more dramatic cases she told us about, they included an assortment of instantly mended fractures, restored sight, and even a severed thumb being reattached without surgery.

We wanted to know the process that Sharon uses, and she explained it this way: She always begins by asking God, Jesus, or His angels to use her as an instrument of healing. Her procedures then vary according to the affliction, and in the case of a localized ailment, she may place her hands directly on that area. If she feels the illness might have emotional or psychological roots, she will then place one hand on the person's forehead and the other on the back of their head just above the neck. She then prays either silently or aloud and remains in this process for quite a while, up to thirty minutes or longer. The person might become aware of deep emotions and may begin to cry, laugh, or express other deep feelings. Sometimes they slump to the floor, and Sharon follows them down to remain in physical contact.

We asked Sharon to come to our house to provide a demonstration, and that was where Linda experienced her dramatic healing from the memory of childhood trauma.[3] (See Chapter 12 for Linda's story.)

THE BODY, SOUL, AND SPIRIT CONNECTION

We found a few prevailing concepts in talking with various people who claim healing gifts similar to Jean's, Tricia's, and Sharon's. There is a tendency to link physical, emotional, and spiritual health as both *causes* and *effects* for one's overall well-being. For example, in stories of physical healing, one often hears the need to first resolve internalized emotional conflicts. The relationship between the body and mind sometimes is easy to see, as in cases of work-related stress and heart attacks. Doctors understand that the fight-or-flight response releases a powerful chemical (adrenaline), which can build up and cause unhealthy stress if we don't exert ourselves in the way our bodies were originally designed to be exercised under threatening situations. Some medical reports now begin to link the effect of emotional stress on weakening the immune system and even on promoting diseases like cancer.

On the other hand, we know that emotional wounds can result from various external causes—accidents, the death of a loved one, divorce, criminal assault, economic loss, layoff, and many other traumas. So the idea of our body, soul, and spirit needing to be considered as a whole being and not treated as separate and unrelated parts appears more than valid.

The concept of *connections* is raised frequently in conversations about healing—not only the connections between body, soul, and spirit—but also the connections between people, through prayer, and healing touch. Perhaps the greatest promise these stories hold is that through the underlying forces of compassion, empathy, and forgiveness, we may witness and experience the inner healing effects of returning to harmony with others, with ourselves, and with the One who created us.

CHAPTER TWENTY

AFTERLIFE EXPERIENCES AND THE RIPPLE EFFECT

I know a man in Christ who fourteen years ago was
caught up to the third heaven. Whether it was in
the body or out of the body I do not know—God
knows. And I know that this man—whether in the
body or apart from the body I do not know, but
God knows—was caught up to paradise. He heard
inexpressible things, things that man is not
permitted to tell. I will boast about a man like that,
but I will not boast about myself, except about my
weaknesses. Even if I should choose to boast, I
would not be a fool, because I would be speaking
the truth. But I refrain, so no one will think more
of me than is warranted by what I do or say.

—2 COR. 12:2–6 NIV

Peter

Throughout the 1990s, I had the great adventure of interviewing many people for TV specials I produced for Discovery's The Learning Channel, including three documentaries: "Life After Life," the two-part "Angel Stories," and another two-part series called "Stories of Miracles." Ultimately, these shows were combined with other interviews and became the Hallmark TV series *Miracles, Angels & Afterlife.*

NEAR-DEATH EXPERIENCES

Some of the most fascinating stories with the greatest insights came during the production of "Life After Life," when I was introduced to several people who had survived near-death experiences (NDEs). We followed the incredible journeys of men and women who had been declared clinically dead. They claimed their consciousness had separated from their bodies, and they found themselves fully aware of their immediate surroundings, even later verifying the activities they'd witnessed in faraway places. Some said they had traveled high above the earth, fully conscious while away from their bodies. Some spoke of traveling down a dark tunnel, frequently encountering deceased loved ones, friends, and relatives. Some said they encountered angelic "beings of light" and heavenly scenes.

Ultimately they found themselves in the presence of a bright, loving—and very personal—Light, whom many identified as Jesus, or The Christ. Others searched for descriptions like Light of God, or Great Being of Light.

After a time with this Light, the departed soul is taken on an epic replay of their entire life, all at once, and down to the last detail.

THE LIFE REVIEW

In one episode of our TV series, we focused on people's encounters with this Light as the climactic element of the NDE. While filming, Dr. Raymond Moody, author of the best-selling book *Life After Life*, made this comment to me about the phenomenon he calls the "life review": "This is one of the most interesting parts of the near-death experience," said Moody. "These patients will tell us that in the closing moments of their life, often in the presence of this 'being of love' who is with them, that they see a panorama before them which consists of every single thing that they've ever done in their lives, from the moment of their birth right through the time of their close call with death. And they say that they see it all simultaneously . . . not with the events in temporal sequence, but rather all displayed there at once in a way that they find very difficult to describe.[1]

Dr. Moody had collected a great number of impressions of the life review in writing *Life After Life*. He gave me a wonderful illustration to describe the feeling one gets by seeing this replay of life, and the conclusions that many people seem to make during this time: "If you imagine this panorama of your life is like a still pond and each action in your life is like a pebble which you flip into that pond . . . at the point where that pebble impacts on the surface, you can see ripples going out.

"But as these ripples in this panorama impinge on others, then you can see the secondary effects going off from those people in the form of ripples. So, I think it illustrates how tied-in we all are to one another in this life . . . how profoundly our actions and our feelings affect others. And, of course, in this life review, we are made aware of that in a very profound way. People say, too, that it's not the big events in your life that you would necessarily expect to be reviewed. It's not the big accomplishments, but rather the simple acts of kindness, often things that you would even have forgotten.[2]

THE RIPPLE EFFECT

This cause-and-effect phenomenon has actually become known in near-death studies as the "ripple effect." In my opinion, it is one of the most profound understandings I have ever gained, confirming some of the most profound teachings of Jesus, which I will discuss shortly. It has affected the way I think about every single thing I do and about my connections with every person on earth. Like ripples in a pond, the unique perspective of the life review allows us to see how our life has intersected with lives of others. In one man's words: "As it started happening, I began to see how I affected the person I had the encounter with . . . and then, in turn, how that encounter affected people who were one step removed from us."[3]

Stowe

One of the fellows Peter interviewed in our home was named Dannion. He was a former military sniper and described reviewing an incident—which had happened many years earlier—when he killed an enemy officer in front of his troops, and the great pride he felt at that moment for the successful hit. He then described simultaneously replaying the very same incident from the point of view of the officer's men, actually feeling their own grief and fear at witnessing their leader gunned down. And for the first time, the soldier actually understood the big picture, from the first-person perspective of the officer's family, when they got news of their loved one's death. He says he could actually feel the emotions of those individual family members (whom he had never seen in life) *as if he were them!* And he could see the ripple effect, through time, of all the subsequent consequences in the lives of the family, all stemming from his single action.[4]

As I listened to this amazing description, I couldn't help but think about the people who had abused me in my childhood—the sadness they would have as they experienced their deeds through my eyes and the ripple effect of those deeds. Somehow I also had an immediate thought about the necessity for me to forgive them, too—as God has forgiven me for things I've done.

On the other hand, I have also heard the same kind of ripple effect describing extremely positive consequences from very small acts of compassion. For example, someone stops to chat with a homeless man, who then decides that perhaps the world is not so cruel after all. As a result, the homeless man resolves to change his life, ultimately getting a job as a gardener at an orphanage, and he becomes a great example of character strength for the children.

The knowledge that I will someday feel the perceptions and emotions of people touched by my life, *as if I were them,* is the most compelling evidence of our spiritual connection and responsibility to one another. I hope, perhaps one day, to understand the connections that have existed between all people throughout all time.

Peter

The life review also seems to demonstrate God's desire for us to understand this connection we share with Him and with each other. I have heard the message from many near-death survivors that while they were watching their emotion-filled life review in the presence of the Lord, they were bathed with a sense of forgiveness for the things about which they felt remorseful or repentant.

The bottom-line question received during their experience was, "In your life, have you learned to love in the way that I love? Did you share love, forgiveness, and compassion in the ways you experience with Me now?" This message resonates with Christ's teachings of loving and forgiving others, as we would have others do to us. The life review, with its supremely important lesson of love, implies profound connections between ourselves, other people, and the God who created us all.

When I began hearing about the all-encompassing life review, it rang a bell with what I've read in the Bible. King Solomon, in the Book of Ecclesiastes, reflects on the value of a person's lifetime and suggests:

> Follow the ways of your heart and whatever your eyes see, but know that for all these things God will bring you to judgment . . . For God will bring every deed into judgment, including every hidden thing, whether it is good or evil. (ECCLES. 11:9, 12:14 NIV)

This sounds similar to the experiences of the people you'll read about in a moment: reviewing every small detail of one's life. Still, I had a hard time reconciling the *loving and forgiving* tone of these near-death experiences with the traditionally held image of judgment, which often goes hand in hand with either the reward of everlasting life or the punishment of eternal damnation. From what I gather from all these accounts, the *Light* of God—the Light of all people, as described in John 1:4–5—is most interested in showing how our lives are interconnected, and how the causes and effects of everything we do are woven into the fabric of His Creation. And during that peculiar circumstance of reviewing our lives, we empathetically feel other people's perceptions and emotions as if we *were* them, while simultaneously reliving our own memory from our own point of view! If indeed we all are connected this way, in Spirit—actually seeing through the eyes and feeling the emotions of others, from a first-person perspective—then the idea of *loving your neighbor as yourself* takes on a whole new and very literal meaning.

It may come as a shock to many of us, when we finally arrive at life's end, to discover that *nobody* has lived a life worthy of God's praises or rewards, regardless of our religious beliefs. I believe it is only because of God's unimaginable grace and mercy that *anyone* and *everyone* has been given a chance to receive His eternal love and forgiveness.

Stowe

EXPERIENCES IN THE LIGHT

Dr. George Ritchie, a wonderful old southern gentleman who was a guest in our home, told us about his glimpse into heaven following a series of strange events. He had "died" from pneumonia, and his spirit had left his body. Finally realizing he was no longer confined to the limits of his physical body, he became bewildered: "Sitting there, I was wondering what to do next, when suddenly the room became flooded with light. And then three things happened simultaneously, just like that," he says, snapping his fingers. "Something deep inside of the spiritual being sitting on the side of the bed, and looking at the corpse lying in the bed, was told to 'stand up, you're in the presence of the Son of God.' Out of that light stepped the most amazing being I have ever been in the presence of . . . the most powerfully built male I have ever seen.

"As those hospital walls virtually disappeared, I saw every minute detail in my life, seeing my own Caesarean-section birth, through the twenty years I had lived (as I was only twenty at the time). And this question was being asked of me, 'What have you done with your life to show me?'

"Well, I'm looking around this panoramic view, and I'm hoping that He'll notice some good things and, of course, I'm trying to pick the best things and hoping He won't see some rather embarrassing things that happened to me as a teenager."

He laughs as he recalls the uncomfortable scenario.

"I thought, *Well, I was an Eagle Scout!*"

Immediately, He responded, "That glorified *you.*"

Again, the question was asked, "What have you done with your life to *show me?*" This time, the emphasis was on "show me."

"But I understood what He was saying. He was asking if I had learned to love my fellow human beings the way He totally accepted and loved me.

"And then—having been in the presence of a being who knows everything about me and knowing He totally accepts me and totally loves me—I never wanted to leave this being again, under any circumstances."[5]

A sweet elderly woman, whom we developed an instant and long-lasting friendship with, explained her version of the life review this way: "With the light there is this panoramic view of my life. It starts with birth, and it continues right on to where we are at this point. I guess it's like a speeded-up version of a camera that just runs double time. And, all at the same time, I am part of the view as well as being able to watch it! I am really doing these things. I actually had the feelings of what was going on as I had seen them, and I also was standing off to the side and able to look around at the different things. I saw things that went on at different times in my life.

"And what I'd always thought was important, and the nice things I had done . . . they didn't even count for anything! It's the little, unknown things you do for one another that count. And love there (as seen from heaven) is always helping to give others a hand along the way. And at the same time you're benefited, because you're receiving, too."[6]

And another man described this insight he gained during his near-death experience: "I had a panoramic view of my life . . . every feeling, every thought, every action, every deed . . . all at the same time. And believe me, there is nothing hidden in your life. You will see the things you did from your heart—helping an old woman, picking a kid up, helping someone else—an action you took, uncalculated, unthought, just out of the goodness of your heart. These things herald through the universe . . . not your great accomplishments . . . not what you achieve or what you think has value. The little things have value.

"And when you look at it, you look at it from a place to review . . . to be critical of yourself, not to be judged or to be condemned. There was no condemnation in it. There was none. There was nothing but, 'Hey look at yourself. Look at who you really are. Look what you've done and then give it a value in the eyes of God.' The death experience gives you a value of what love really is . . . that you are so deeply loved and that you yourself can so deeply love. You begin to sense a part of yourself greater and far more magnificent than you ever gave yourself credit for."[7]

For every action there is a reaction; for every choice, a consequence. We rarely know life's destination until we arrive, and we cannot predict where the ripples go from the stones we cast into life's waters. But, if we use God's love as the basis for all our actions, we can be assured that the ripples sent out will be ones that we'll want returned to us later.

Peter

I interviewed another fascinating man for the Hallmark Channel show *Miracles, Angels & Afterlife*. Henry had a near-death experience with some very interesting side effects.

HENRY SMILEY

"The day after Thanksgiving in 1993, my family and I were visiting the home of some out-of-town friends. At 1:30 or so in the morning, my thirteen-month-old daughter had awakened and wanted a bottle of milk. So I proceeded very groggily to the kitchen, which was situated near a stairwell that led directly into the basement. Returning from the kitchen, I would have to dogleg around the stairwell in order to move back to the guest bedroom where the light was on.

"I was so half-asleep that—with the bottle of milk in my hand—I looked at the light, and instead of walking around the stairwell, I walked directly into that stairwell of seventeen stairs and proceeded to tumble down the flight.

"Shortly thereafter, I became fully conscious again, but now I was in a setting of complete calm and tranquility, as you may have heard about in other near-death experiences— with absolute compassion surrounding me and no anxiety whatsoever. I was approached by two oval shapes of light. The closer of these two lights spoke to me in a very feminine voice, asking if I would like to go forward or would I like to go back.

"And I said, 'Well, I have a young daughter that I'm very connected to and I would like to be in her life. I would like to be a father to this child.' The immediate answer was that my wife and my daughter would be completely fine if I chose to go forward to the next realm. 'Well, if you're giving me a choice . . .' I said, without feeling any anxiety about it, 'I would like to go back and be a father to her.' At that she said, 'You may go back, but just know that you will have to deal with the physical trauma of your accident.' I said, 'That'll be fine.' And with that, I blinked and came to.

"I found myself in a hospital bed. I was fully conscious, back in my body, and saw my wife and friends sitting there. I said, 'I'm back.'

"Upon my release from the hospital, I went back to my friends' house and spent some incredible moments with my thirteen-month-old daughter. For about half an hour we had a connection that was just incredible. From that time on, there was another purpose . . . not just to be a father to her, but to pass on some of the mystery of my experience and some of the evolution of the whole spiritual process that I saw firsthand. This has been truly phenomenal."[8]

Something unusual seems to happen to the survivors of near-death experiences after they've passed through that veil, so to speak, between earth and heaven. These people who've glimpsed eternity often have a different perspective of *time*, as we know it. They often speak of seeing future visions that may involve prophetic insights into world events. But sometimes these insights take on a more personal scope. Henry described one scene he recalls from his glimpse into eternity, which involved his little daughter.

"I have an indelible picture of seeing my daughter as an elderly lady. She's lying in bed late at night, remembering all the love that had grown and developed during our family life. I'm not in her life any longer. I have passed on. My wife has passed on. My daughter's husband has passed on. But the beautiful thing about the picture was that there was no sadness; she felt so fulfilled because of the compassion . . . not only which we discovered together, but which she had taken and built upon in her life and then passed along to other people."[9]

I heard someone describe this ability to see through portals in time, so to speak, as being comparable to modern digital technology. On a digital hard drive, which is the memory bank of every computer, information is stored in a nonlinear way; that is, it exists all at once, in a dimension unrelated to time. However, it is normally only retrieved and seen by people in a linear way, from the beginning to the end, in continuity.

In the same way, eternity might be thought of as existing all at once, as another dimension beyond linear time. When someone gets a peek into the past or future, as Henry describes, they may be somehow accessing a nonlinear dimension we refer to as *eternity*.

Another side effect that often accompanies a near-death experience is the development of a *telepathic* or *empathic* ability to "read" people. In some ways it resembles the description of the life review during an NDE, where one feels the emotions of other people they encountered in life. This extrasensitivity often follows one's brush with death, and may at first seem baffling to those who begin picking up spontaneous insights into other people's lives.

Henry Smiley began to develop this ability following his near-death experience. He explains: "I was moved to begin daily meditation after the NDE without knowing why I was being propelled to do so. I just did it! I spent time clearing my mind, and these intuitive insights would emerge, eventually becoming a part of my life on an ongoing basis."

His glimpses into the lives of others have become an unusual gift, which he uses in a low-key way to assist people, even when they don't know they need it. I witnessed a vivid example of this myself the very first time I met Henry.

LUCKY GUESS?

I had been invited to a local library to do a signing session for my book *Reflections of Heaven*, and to present a few video clips of our TV shows. Following the program, I began mingling with the audience. One fellow, who had shown an interest in NDEs during the presentation, came up and introduced himself to me. We exchanged business cards. His card read HENRY SMILEY, CREATIVE CONSULTANT. He told me about his own near-death experience and was just beginning to tell me about a peculiar ability that he had developed as a result, when we were suddenly interrupted.

The crowds were shifting, and while I was signing someone else's book, Henry began a conversation with another member of the audience. Although Henry and I never finished our conversation that evening, I was eager to hear what he had to say. So the next day I called the phone number on his business card.

"What I was going to say," Henry continued, "is that since my near-death experience, I have become somewhat empathetic with other individuals. For instance, while listening to your presentation last night, a gentleman sitting behind me—

whom I had not yet met or even turned around to look at—raised his hand and asked you a question. As soon as I heard his voice, I knew that there would be some information that I would need to pass on to him.

"In fact, I spoke to him after the meeting," Henry said, "and I learned his name was Denny. As soon as we began talking I sensed two names very strongly. One name was Mary and the other was Margaret. Mary turned out to be his sister and Margaret was a lady he worked with. As soon as he said his sister's name was Mary, I saw an image of a female with a physical problem on the left side of her body that was causing problems while she was walking. I asked Denny, 'Is your sister having trouble with the left side of her body?'

"And Denny said, 'I don't know because we haven't talked in quite some time.'

"And then," Henry added, "the Holy Spirit also shared with me that Denny and his sister had a long-standing sibling rivalry, and that there was a wound in the heart between the two of them. So I suggested that Denny call Mary to see how she's feeling."

Henry and I chatted a while longer, then we wrapped up our call. A week later at another book-signing, to my surprise, a member of the audience introduced himself as Denny, the same fellow Henry had mentioned. He had come to share the amazing follow-up to Henry's story.

Denny stood up to share with the new audience. "I met a man named Henry Smiley last week at another of Mr. Shockey's book-signings. He asked me, out of the blue, if I knew anyone named Margaret or Mary. . . ."

Denny went on to tell about Henry's insight into his sister Mary's left hip. Then he added, "I called her up that night, and darn if it wasn't true. In fact, she had just been to a doctor who'd found a bone spur on her left hip, and they discussed surgery."

Denny said the following thirty-minute conversation with his sister was the longest they'd had in quite a long while, and was also the most loving and compassionate. She had softened from her usual defensiveness with her brother because her interpretation of the event was, "You cared enough to call me."[10]

Since witnessing that encounter between Henry and Denny firsthand, I've learned of other incidents in which Henry uses his insights to offer "creative consultation" to help people—often in quite unexpected ways.

One man who survived an NDE shared an interesting illustration for what he believes is behind this kind of sensitivity. Something that caught my attention was his depiction of the Holy Spirit.

"In a dream," he explained, "I was shown an overlapping grid, or matrix, that surrounded the earth. And I was shown the grid with the understanding that every fact, every thought, every bit of knowledge that has ever emanated from this planet, and will ever emanate from this planet from any individual, resides in that grid. There are similar references in some religious writings to a great library of knowledge called the Akashic Records. In Jewish, Christian, and Islamic texts, a similar idea of a detailed record is referred to as the Book of Life. In this case it was shown to me as a grid. I think the Holy Spirit empowers this grid through us, so when we open up to the compassion of the Spirit, we are allowed to intersect with it and to access this information.

"I began to realize that every day in which I spend time reducing the concerns of my own ego-driven demands, I start feeling the larger connections of life around me; and not just with my immediate family and closest friends, but I begin to feel a kinship through this Holy Spirit—connecting us with the larger sphere of life."[11]

Please forgive my taking creative license, but to understand the Spirit does take an expanded vocabulary, and a "grid" that connects people to God works for me in the same way that Jesus' metaphor of the "vine" describes a similar concept. Consider these excerpts from John 15:

> "I am the true vine and my Father is the gardener. . . . I am the vine; you are the branches. If a man remains in me and I in him, he will bear much fruit; apart from me he can do nothing. . . . If you remain in me and my words remain in you, ask whatever you wish, and it will be given you. As the Father has loved me, so have I loved you. Now remain in my love. If you obey my commands, you will remain in my love, just as I have obeyed my Father's commands and remained in his love. . . . My command is this: Love each other as I have loved you. . . ."
>
> (JOHN 15:5, 7, 9–12 NIV)

And a few paragraphs later, Jesus speaks about more of these profound connections of the Spirit:

> "When the Counselor comes, whom I will send to you from the Father—the Spirit of truth who goes out from the Father—he will testify about me. . . . But, when he, the Spirit of truth, comes, he will guide you into all truth. He will not speak on his own; he will speak only what he hears and will tell you what is yet to come."
>
> (JOHN 15:26; 16:13 NIV)

Updating the agricultural metaphor of the vine to the information age, I do get a picture of a grid, or a living network of living and breathing creations—in other words *us*—in which God's Holy Spirit may dwell. A line unplugged from the power source is just as cut off and lifeless as a branch apart from the vine. And the Holy Spirit, when thought of as God's very own breath—the spark of life itself—is the energy that powers the network of life. Furthermore, when a communication grid, like the Internet, is working as designed, it can pass messages from the sender, just as *"the Spirit of truth . . . will speak only what he hears, and he will tell you what is yet to come"* (John 16:13–14 NIV).

FLIPPING THE SWITCH

I was given another interesting image by Henry Smiley. He didn't travel to a faraway place this time, but deep within his own body and into the microcosm of his own DNA. As the vision unfolded, Henry traveled down a long helical spiral with the genetically encoded information whizzing past at a fantastic rate. Sequences flew by that determined the color of his skin, the tint of his eyes, the size of his skeleton, and the health of every organ.

He saw and somehow understood which of the encoded patterns determined his inheritance of a strong ear for music and his weakness for other skills. Finally, in this dream, he was shown a particular genetic sequence, highlighted "like a special-effect, 3-D animation" to show the specific code dealing with spiritual sensitivity. Henry says he understood this sequence functions like an "on-off" switch that hormonally regulates our mind and body in relation to the awareness of our spirit. He gathered that the switch is usually inherited in the "off" position and typically requires a conscious and willful decision to turn it to the "on" position.

Smiley hypothesized that certain experiences might have the effect of resetting the switch to its original default position—in which the natural perception of the spiritual realm is left "on"—much like turning a computer off and then on again to reset its programs to the default mode.[12]

Again, this was just one man's vision, and I don't mean to give it too much scientific or spiritual weight; but it gives an interesting model of what some call humanity's inherited sinful nature. My thoughts on this subject come back to the unforgettable encounter I had as a young man with Christ's living Spirit, in which I experienced a total restoration of my awareness of a previously unknown realm. It was as if I had been blind and suddenly could see.

It truly appears to me that people are born with their spiritual awareness of God in the "off" position! Born (as most seem to be) without a consciousness of their relationship to God or to others, people naturally behave as if they were the sole centers of their universe . . . until they choose to allow that Light to enter. This is what I believe we commonly call humanity's "fallen" condition.

Perhaps one day, after sufficient generations of individuals have willingly turned their spiritual lights "on"—being *reborn of the Spirit*—there may come a time when humanity develops (or perhaps *re*develops) that inherited consciousness of God's glory.

And I will give you a new heart with new and right desires, and I will put a new spirit in you. I will

take out your stony heart of sin and give you a new,
obedient heart. And I will put my Spirit in you so
you will obey my laws and do whatever I
command . . . You will be my people,
and I will be your God.

—EZEK. 36:26–28 NLT

CHAPTER TWENTY-ONE

THE RIPPLE EFFECT

Light can journey infinite distances when
unobstructed.
Miracles can happen . . . in a flash.
Where Light penetrates darkness, life continues;
But, where Light is blocked, life dies.
What we experience in our life, is God's Light,
traveling through the dense stuff of the material
plane. . . .

The greatest resistance to God's Light in this world
is the human will,
which requires only our decision to unblock.
Once we willfully decide to let our egos be
transparent,
we become conduits and conductors for His Light,
to journey into—and ripple through—
the medium of our life.

Stowe

This book wouldn't have been a complete story unless we had told you about the people we've met—people from whom we have learned so much. But we saved our most special traveling companions for last—our children.

CHRISTINA AND GRACE

A few years ago our family was driving home from a lakeside vacation in Arkansas when we stopped for dinner at a road-side restaurant. As the motherly waitress brought our water, our four-year-old daughter Christina struck up a conversation.

"I'm going to be a paleontologist when I grow up!" reported Christina.

"A what?" replied the woman.

"A dinosaur hunter. I like looking for their bones."

"Oh, I see!" the waitress smiled, looking sideways at me and nodding. I nodded back, proud of my little girl's vocabulary.

"And I know how they became ek-stink!" said Christina.

The woman's lips puckered and her eyes widened as she nodded again toward my daughter as if to say, "All right then, tell me."

"A billion years ago, a giant meat-eater [she meant "meteor"] fell down on the earth. It covered the world in darkness, and everything caught cold and died." Christina's voice took on great authority as she continued, "And now, their bones can only be found in Vir-Geornia and New-Hamster."

Now, I don't know if the waitress enjoyed that paleontology lesson as much as we did, but we boasted the story to our friends for weeks, and each time we shared it I felt more proud of my little dinosaur hunter.

Peter
And then there's Grace, our youngest, who has turned out to be perfectly named. At such a tender age, she shows God's love in countless ways. Stowe and I are constantly comparing notes

about how Grace shows her sensitivity to others through things she does and says. Once, when she was much younger, she had a little accident in the middle of the night, which was rare. She was very upset, and Stowe helped her to get changed and back to sleep. The next afternoon, without prompting, she went to Stowe and said, "Mommy, I want to say *'thank you'* for helping me with my sheets and everything last night." She gave Stowe a big hug, and then ran off to play.

Those moments with our girls, and a million more, are what make life wonderful. And I count each memory with the people I love as the most important events in my life. These are the times that add up to making our journey not only beautiful, but heavenly.

DROPPING THE STONE

So how do we know how many people that waitress told the dinosaur story to after we left that day? How many people got a chuckle and then passed the story along to someone else? And how will Stowe's act of helping our daughter with her bedsheets, which didn't seem like a "favor" to Stowe but the most natural thing in the world for a mother to do, affect how Grace will treat her own children? How will that simple act of kindness pass on to her children's children?

We have no way of knowing the answers to these questions. Maybe the answer is: It doesn't matter. What matters is that every thing we do, no matter how insignificant or how grandiose it might seem at the moment, is like a stone that falls into the water. Tiny concentric rings form around the event and expand to greater circles until . . . well, who knows when? The point is that our simple words or actions may be the stone that falls, but the ripples from that stone extend far beyond our understanding.

We counted on the beauty of the ripple effect when we began writing this book. We hoped the stories we shared would heal and inspire others to drop their stones into life's pond, and that their stories, in turn, would heal and inspire others, and on and on. It worked out far better than we ever prayed it would. For example, I gave a copy of my book *Reflections of Heaven* to a young man named Todd, a talented classical guitarist. He was stirred by one of the stories in the book and felt inspired to share one of his own stories with us. This is a beautiful illustration of how one story can open a heart and inspire someone to share their own personal treasure—like this one:

FOR ERICA

"I belong to a Gypsy song and dance troupe called Labyrinthe. Our old drummer, Clay Plunk, lived in a German-style castle he and his father built, which was also the site for his Drachenburg Renaissance Festival. Every other Sunday, Clay would host a musical event at his home. One Sunday we were playing for a castle full of people, and I noticed a little girl intently watching me.

"After performing a song called "Charmer," the little girl yelled, 'Again!' We all laughed, and then her mother announced, 'That's really quite a compliment because, you see, my daughter is deaf!' Throughout the rest of the performance, the little girl didn't take her eyes off me and my guitar. She was watching so intently I was almost uncomfortable.

"After we finished, I was getting a bite to eat when the little girl came to me and started signing. I felt bad because I didn't know how to sign and couldn't communicate with her. Her mother kindly translated for me. She said her daughter's name was Erica and that she was complimenting my guitar-playing.

"This spawned an idea—a way I could confidently communicate with Erica. I led the little girl into the family room where others were eating and conversing. I sat her down, got my guitar out, and I sat next to her. Then I took her hand and placed it flat onto the face of my guitar. As soon as I started playing, Erica began to grin from ear to ear. I played for forty-five minutes or so, and Erica, smiling the whole time, didn't once move her hand. Erica's parents loved seeing her so happy. Apparently the girl was quite ill with a serious stomach condition.

"During the following week, I thought back to little Erica— deaf, but so interested in something musical. She'd left such an impression on me.

"On Thursday of that week, Clay's wife, Tina, called me. She was crying so hard I could barely understand her. Erica was rushed to the hospital, where they found that her heart had swollen. But the local hospital was not equipped to deal with it, so a LifeFlight helicopter had taken her to Vanderbilt Children's Hospital. Early that morning, during the helicopter ride, little Erica passed away. All this happened in just a matter of days after meeting her—for the first and last time. I was very sad.

"Tina told me Erica's parents requested that I play at the funeral, which was to be the next Sunday (exactly one week after meeting Erica at the castle). Erica's mother said all little Erica talked about the last few days of her life was the 'guy with the guitar' and how much she wanted to learn to play.

"That's the part that got to me. My eyes welled up.

"I not only agreed to play at the funeral, but I also offered to compose an original piece—just for Erica. I would only play the piece once in public, and that would be at the funeral of this precious little girl.

"Sunday found us all mournful in a way that only the death of a child can do. At the funeral, I was sitting in the loft where I would be playing the short classical piece I'd written: "For Erica." Rachel Sullivan, a singer friend of ours, was there with me. She was supposed to sing "Amazing Grace" before I played. How she got through it without breaking down, I'll never know. As Rachel sang, I looked to my side and considered the words of the song.

"Then I noticed soft light coming through a window, while the dust in the air created a light-beam effect. I followed the light down, slowly . . . slowly . . . slowly . . . until I realized the beam of light stopped upon the surface of my guitar, which was sitting at my side.

"My eyes widened as I realized what I was seeing. The way the beam of light was resting on my guitar, I could plainly see a tiny ghost of a handprint—Erica's handprint from the week before—there on the face of my guitar."[1]

Therefore we do not lose heart. Even though our outward man is perishing, yet the inward man is being renewed day by day. For our light affliction, which is but for a moment, is working for us a far more exceeding and eternal weight of glory, while we do not look at the things which are seen, but at the things which are not seen. For the things which are seen are temporary, but the things which are not seen are eternal.

—2 COR. 4:16–18 NKJV

THANKSGIVING AND PRAISE

Peter

Stowe's and my life together, like so many others in today's world, is now in a different chapter of history—especially since the events of September 11, 2001, and what has followed. Many things have changed for many people. Some may feel a bit less financially secure. Others feel less safe and more vulnerable to danger. Many people like us take better daily account of our priorities—how we spend our time and resources. And like many others in this unstable world, I am increasingly aware of how interconnected we all are. It's hard to believe anything good could have come from the historical events that rocked our world. But since that time, more people have come to realize how one person's actions can affect the lives of so many others.

Looking back at how I felt when we first started writing this book, I'm very happy to say that I personally no longer feel I'm living under a dark cloud. Whatever it was I had felt creeping into my soul during those months of uncertainty—call it fear, depression, angst, whatever the name—it lost its grip on me. I can't recall when it left, or just what made it go. But I know that I prayed a lot, taking my anxieties to God and asking His guidance. I prayed for the Lord to heal the disconnection I felt from so many aspects of my life and from Him. And, most importantly, I never stopped counting our blessings.

Stowe

Counting our blessings is always a sure way of reconnecting to God. I love Psalm 100, which describes how to come into the Lord's presence using the floor plan of the Temple as a metaphor; "*Enter His gates with* thanksgiving *and His courts with* praise" (v. 4 NASB; emphasis mine). Once inside the inner courtyard, the ancient priest could enter the Holy of Holys, where God's Spirit resided, and could commune with Him. The Bible then makes an extraordinary leap when we read, "*Do you not know that you are God's temple and that God's Spirit dwells in you?*" (1 Cor. 3:16 ESV). Did you realize that you can enter the place where God's Holy Spirit dwells, to reconnect with His eternal Light, without having to set foot in a temple made of bricks and mortar? You *are* the temple, and you *hold the keys!* The spiritual keys to enter God's holy place, in our hearts, are *praise* and *thanksgiving*.

Praise is easy enough to understand; we simply acknowledge the goodness in someone. Webster defines it as *an expression of warm approval or admiration*. It doesn't necessarily have to come out as "Praise You, Lord" (although that can be a good warm-up), but it does involve telling God all the wonderful things you recognize about Him and what He is doing in the Universe, which He is continuing to create for us and, if we allow Him, through us.

And thanksgiving? It's as simple as being thankful for every thing, and recognizing it . . . and that's what we do when we count our blessings. We acknowledge what God has done, and we thank Him for it.

How unnecessarily shut out we are from God's presence when we adopt an attitude of counting our *problems* instead of our *blessings*. Just like the way Peter's and my hearts are touched when our daughter Grace says "Thank you," God must also be delighted when His children reconnect with Him by taking the time to say "Thanks."

> *Rejoice always; pray without ceasing; in everything*
> *give thanks; for this is God's will for you in Christ*
> *Jesus.*
>
> —1 THESS. 5:16–18 NASB

THE ULTIMATE RECONNECTION

If you've never read the first chapter of John's Gospel, it contains the entire story of the journey of Light—the creation of every thing by the Word through the Light of God. Our spark of life through His Spirit, which is the Light of life. Our disconnection from that Light by our own ignorance. The Light's return to the world in the person of Jesus. And the spiritual link, which Christ provided to reconnect us as God's children—children of Light (see also 1 Thess. 5:5). Listen to the story as it has been told to countless offspring:

In the beginning was the Word, and the Word was with God, and the Word was God. He was with God in the beginning. Through him all things were made; without him nothing was made that has been made. In him was life, and that life was the light of men. The light shines in the darkness, but the darkness has not understood it. There came a man who was sent from God; his name was John. He came as a witness to testify concerning that light, so that through him all men might believe. He himself was not the light; he came only as a witness to the light. The true light that gives light to every man was coming into the world. He was in the world, and though the world was made through him, the world did not recognize him. He came to that which was his own, but his own did not receive him. Yet to all who received him, to those who believed in his name, he gave the right to become children of God—children born not of natural descent, nor of human decision or a husband's will, but born of God. The Word became flesh and made his dwelling among us. We have seen his glory, the glory of the One and Only, who came from the Father, full of grace and truth. (JOHN 1–14 NIV)

Of course, for many people this is only the beginning of the story. The story is the journey of *God's Light,* traveling through the lives of all who allow Him. And it is a story that by its own nature will never end.

NOTES

Chapter Eight

1. Marietta Jaeger, interview by Peter Shockey, *News Odyssey*, June 3, 1999.

Chapter Eleven

1. Roger Sperry, Nobel lecture, December 8, 1981; http://nobelprize.org/ medicine/laureates/1981/sperry-lecture.html (accessed June 7, 2006).

2. Joseph Hellige, *Hemispheric Asymmetry: What's Right and What's Left,* Harvard University Press; http://www.powells.com/cgibin/biblio?inkey=17- 0674387309-0 (accessed June 7, 2006).

3. Alfred and Evelyn Bennett, interview by Peter Shockey, Nolensville, Tennessee, January 14, 2000.

Chapter Twelve

1. Interview with "Linda," by Peter Shockey, Nashville, Tennessee, September 10, 1999.

Chapter Thirteen

1. Jean Bertram, interview by Stowe D. Shockey, February 15, 2000.

Chapter Fifteen

1. William Claiborne, "Recovering Farrakhan Urges Unity, Forgiveness," *Washington Post,* December 23, 1999, p. A-04.

2. Ibid.

3. Ibid.

4. Ibid.

Chapter Sixteen

1. John Fletcher, *Studies on Slavery, in Easy Lessons,* originally published in a slightly different form (Miami: Mnemosyne, 1969; Natchez, 1852), pp. 435–77. Quoted in Smith, *In His Image,* p. 131. See also Nathan Lord, *A Letter of Inquiry to Ministries of the Gospel of All Denominations on Slavery* (Hanover, NH: n.p., 1861), pp. 5–6.

2. Lee McRee, interview by Peter Shockey, Thompson Station, Tennessee, April 10, 2002.

Chapter Eighteen

1. Judy McDonald, interview by Stowe D. Shockey, Nolensville, Tennessee, March 6, 2000.

2. Arch Anthony Dawson, interview with Fred Rowles by Peter Shockey, *Miracles, Angels & Afterlife,* Odyssey TV series, Nashville, Tennessee, September 5, 2000.

3. Dick Drehmer, interview by Peter Shockey, Princeton, Massachusetts, July 10, 2000.

4. Todd and Sherry Beezley, interview by Stowe D. Shockey, Nolensville, Tennessee, August 1, 2000.

Chapter Nineteen

1. Jean Bertram, interview by Stowe D. Shockey, February 15, 2000.

2. Tricia McMahon, interview by Peter Shockey, Nashville, Tennessee, December 12, 2000.

3. Sharon Forrest, interview by Peter Shockey, *Miracles, Angels & Afterlife*, Odyssey TV series, Nashville, Tennessee, September 5, 2000.

Chapter Twenty

1. Raymond Moody, M.D., interview by Peter Shockey, "Life After Life," The Learning Channel show, Nashville, Tennessee, February 29, 1992.

2. Ibid.

3. Dannion Brinkley, interview by Peter Shockey, "Life After Life," The Learning Channel show, Nashville, Tennessee, February 28, 1992.

4. Ibid.

5. Dr. George Ritchie, interview by Peter Shockey, "Life After Life," The Learning Channel show, Nashville, Tennessee, February 18, 1992.

6. Viola Horton, interview by Peter Shockey, "Life After Life," The Learning Channel show, Nashville, Tennessee, February 28, 1992.

7. Ibid.

8. Henry Smiley, interview by Peter Shockey, *Miracles, Angels & Afterlife*, Odyssey TV series, Nashville, Tennessee, August 17, 2000.

9. Ibid.

10. Ibid.

11. Ibid.

12. Ibid.

Chapter Twenty-one

1. Todd Kirby, personal message to author, "For Erica," unpublished, sent November 12, 2002.

PERMISSIONS

Scripture quotations are taken from the following sources:

The American Standard Version (ASV) of the Holy Bible. Public domain.

Contemporary English Version® (CEV). Copyright © 1995 by American Bible Society. Used by permission.

The Holy Bible, English Standard Version (ESV). Copyright © 2001 by Crossway Bibles, a division of Good News Publishers. Used by permission. All rights reserved.

The Holman Christian Standard Bible® (HCSB). Copyright © 1999, 2000, 2002, 2003 by Holman Bible Publishers. All rights reserved.

The New American Standard Bible® (NASB). Copyright © 1960, 1962, 1963, 1968, 1971, 1972, 1973, 1975, 1977, 1995 by The Lockman Foundation. Used by permission.